The Path of the Creator

The Path of the Creator

A Guided Journey Towards Oneness

Theo Salvucci

Received by Theo Salvucci

There will be no time at all in which anyone incarnate will be
authorized to conduct a workshop or any other group, or give a lecture
based on this book, either for free or for recompense.

10th edition © Copyright 2012 by Theo Salvucci
Printed in the United States of America.

Library of Congress PCN Data
Lenonda (Spirit)
The path of the Creator :
a guided journey towards oneness with all that is /
Theo Salvucci.
p. cm.
ISBN 9780982786161 (pbk.)
1. Spirit writings. I. Salvucci, Theo, 1952- II. Title.

Thanks to Brian and Pam
of Granite Publishing, for their
long-time support
in getting this project launched.

Address all inquiries to:
THEOS Press
33 Ravencroft Lane
Asheville, NC 28803

http://www.theosalvucci.com

THEOS Press walks lightly on the Earth.

Thank you,
everyone,
for your support and help.

Table of Contents

Book Two

Theo Salvucci

Foreword

*T*he *Path of the Creator* first came in outline form during one of my channeled workshops in Asheville, North Carolina, in March of 1996. It had been promised to me by my principal guide Lenonda some months prior. As I have been channeling since August of 1990 and begun holding channeled gatherings in July of 1994, it seems to me to have been a long time in coming. However, I know that the work is timed to make best use of my own spiritual growth and the path of the book's potential readers.

Perhaps a word about what channeling is would be in order.

Channeling is everyone's innate ability. We each have an ongoing connection to God that not only energizes and inspires us, but also informs our essence. We are beings who are created and recreated every moment. We may participate in this creation or we may deny the process and surrender to God, even a God whom we hold in disbelief. But our connection must be constant, as there are no true continua.

As if tracing ourselves back to our Source, we can find in our search for God a hidden aspect of self which we can call the higher self. It forms a separate consciousness and is alive on a separate plane of existence into which we merge when we pass from this earthly plane. The higher self, in this path to the Creator, ultimately serves as a guide for our lives. It is a link to even higher states of soul that become more elusive in identity, until we can no longer speak of self as apart from God.

It is a sine qua non that a channel has connection to this higher self. It may have happened through arduous spiritual work or may have appeared to come about effortlessly, but this connection is quite necessary. From this merging of consciousness, channeling begins. If you can imagine that one's alignment to God is on a vertical axis, channeling crosses this axis with a horizontal one at the point of the higher self, enabling communication with that self's world, be it by thought, imagery, sensation, or word. As we sit in our earthly plane speaking to and learning from the beings in our milieu, the higher self does so also. And at the juncture between our selves, we can speak about beings whom we call our guides or guardian angels.

After prayer and meditation, but without the necessity of going into a trance, the channel, routing his consciousness through that of his higher self, is able to form a bridge for communication. The entity being channeled merges then with the consciousness and the physical body of the channel. Emotions and sensations accompany this union. It is, of course, most important to connect in love, so heart feelings are sought out by the channel. At some point after recognition and acceptance of the being as one of love, imagery pops into the channel's mind, as well as thoughts or sensations. In the higher planes, sensations are more intense but not as succinct as our own, and so imagery is packed with meaning. The entity, with the channel's help, then translates all that into the channel's own language, using the channel's own lexicon and style, and stimulating the body and speech centers to convey the personality in posture or gestures. At no time is a conscious channel unaware or not in control of what is coming out of his mouth. This is both a blessing and a curse. For, while there is never a feeling of being manipulated, and while the channel could always censor what is being said or question it before it is spoken, fear in the channel can also impede the process. In fact, I would say that the elimination of fear is the ongoing healing necessary to be completely open to channeling.

All of this is not to say that there are not dangers associated with channeling, for, as there is Light, there is also darkness. It has been my practice to ask for God's protection and to ask God alone to send me only beings of Light and love. And it is an absolute necessity to feel the heart energy—the energy of love that stimulates one's own loving heart—before allowing channeling to take place. This has been the case with all of the many beings channeled in The Path of the Creator.

It is also possible for our ordinary selves to interfere with the message. I think that is the reason for the seemingly slow pace of my own development. I have been through a great number of healings and cleansings in the past few years. I would hope that you find The Path of the Creator to be devoid of immodesty, projection, or egocentrism. In any event, this is why I say channels must anchor their consciousness in the consciousness of their own higher selves in order to avoid the smallness of the earthly personality.

My principal guide, an angelic being named Lenonda, introduces the book and facilitates my connection to the many beings who are channeled in it. Each chapter is channeled by a different entity. There is a purpose in this: to express the vastness of life in the universe. Life stretches to infinity and we can see this by experiencing enough of its expressions. It has been refreshing to encounter so many different beings in spirit at this time on Earth, when even the simple difference of human skin color can cause division and oppression. I hope that in this book, I have been able to translate what I have seen as a great, diverse universe full of life in uncountable varieties, as well as a universe of inherent love. God, after all, despises sameness and conformity and loves all equally. I would hope that you would feel like adding your own self to this list of souls.

When I have channeled animals, I have done so with angelic assistance and sometimes connected to their oversoul or group soul, which they all have and we all have. The nature spirits or devas speak for themselves, as do human or human-like souls and those of the angelic kingdom. I received much assistance in channeling our Creator.

One might notice that each of the seven archangels who have to do with our realm of existence is represented in the Path. I have borrowed these names because they have a certain rhyming consistency, although each of them has many names. Other proper names will be familiar to the reader, and I make no apologies for the unorthodox spiritual guidance received from them. However, I trust that the reader will find that the thread of truth is apparent, and that this truth binds together what has been diverse mythology in a loving manner. There are many allusions in the Path, some more apparent than others; yet, once again it may be just as simple and more accepting in love to see their connective truth as more sustaining than to focus on their succinct interpretations which often serve merely to sustain the worldly power of their respective religions.

It is a peculiarity of souls who attain higher states of consciousness to lose much of the primitive thoughts of ego or self, seeing themselves in context always to those beings of like kind and to the universe. There simply is no word in our language that expresses "I" while acknowledging "we," and so I have simply allowed the irregularity of shifting from one word to the other as seems fit. Please understand that these consciousnesses are unlike our own common minds.

Another peculiarity of this channeled book is that it is in the second person. I received this form with much trust and believe that Lenonda's purpose—for it is her book, not mine—has been to avoid masculine-by-preference storytelling. It is also the case that, in this way, each chapter can be experienced by the reader as a kind of dialogue. And, perhaps as you read, you may thus summon to yourself the healing energies of these beings, if not their very presence.

The words used in the book are part of my own vocabulary. Everything except this forward has been channeled directly by me onto tape and later transcribed. I subsequently edited the verbatim transcription, eliminating false starts, and deleting repetitions which only made sense in oral communication. I corrected a few grammatical errors, and substituted synonyms, streamlining sentence structure for the sake of better prose. If I had a question about a word or phrase, I later channeled an explanation or got permission to change something. But, this was rare. By far, most of the changes were with the words themselves, for instance substituting "immense" for "great" or "pinnacle" for "top," to avoid redundancy and also to find the truest expression of the channeled thought.

As I have indicated, it is impossible to divorce the channeling from one's own personality. In connecting to my higher self I hope that, my personality is of a higher order, generous of heart, clearminded, and faithful to the truth. And I saw this as my responsibility, but it is a personality, nevertheless, and not an end all and be all of sublime communication. I cannot claim to be an experienced author, and I imagine this will show to some extent. I can only trust that my guidance is wiser than I am, and that I have indeed received Divine guidance, and that there can be good purpose to everything created.

Thank you for your willingness to take a path of love.

Introduction

We bring you greetings from the Source of All Light and Love. My name is Lenonda, and I am here to help instruct you in this era of Earth's great changes. At this time, Earth's critical mass is culminating. Critical mass is that which is neither of Light nor darkness. Critical mass is energy whose origins are God and yet will not lead you directly into the Light, but will propel you, according to your own hearts, in whatever direction you choose. Consequently, you must be firm in what you believe. You must be confident in your purpose, and you must be true to the Light, to the will of God. Then you will see that the will of God is really your will, or that your will is an element of God. But you need to know that the components, which are in place at this time to help you move into a higher state of consciousness, have taken on grand properties and enormous magnitude and scope, and that these energies can either hurl you into the darkness, if that is what your heart wishes, or into the Light. Remember this: there is always a capability and a propensity to embrace darkness as well as Light in all beings of free will. We, as beings of Light and Love, do not wish you to go into darkness. So, how do we help you on your spiritual path?

At the present time, we want you to sit in your center when you are reading, when you are engaging in play, when you are worshiping, when you are doing all of your daily activities. We ask, especially since we have reached this critical period, that when you read anything pertaining to the spirit, you stay in your own center. This center is one of love, because love runs through the core of your being. It is not the center of mind, because you do not always know that you have a mind. It is not the center of joy, although it is quite fine to be in joy. It is not the center of knowing who you are, knowing your higher properties, or knowing your soul. It is knowing that there is love and that love is finding expression in the body. The body is in need of being centered as well as mind. The mind is only centered when the body is. You know that, if you have experienced discomfort in the body, there is a need to ease the discomfort for the mind to function well. Likewise, if you are engaged in an activity that is to give you joy and your heart is not in it, this activity ends up creating sadness in you.

So, what we are telling you in all this is to sit down and feel the love. If you wait until you feel love coming in to you, not phony love, but true core feelings of love without judgment, without pretense, without extraneous stimuli or the stimulus of memory, and simply sit in a loving centered state, you will fulfill your prerequisite for reading this book. It is not important to have achieved something spiritually. It is not important to be in meditation. It is not necessary to be a certain way along your path or to have been a certain kind of conscious being. It is simply necessary to stay in love, read in love, and act in love.

Now, despite the structure of your society that has conferred knowledge on you, we ask your permission to pretend that you are a fool who knows nothing. Embrace the fool. The fool knows only that the fool is alive and does not have a rationale for why it is alive. The fool knows only that it is living and that it must have some good purpose, because life is so wonderful. There is joy in being alive. This is you. You are the fool. You are the fool who has traveled and yet has gone nowhere. In this book you will be the fool again who will travel and will have gone nowhere. You will see that you are the fool, because so many of the fool's attributes seem to be yours.

If you begin the book with some pretense of knowledge, some egotism, or some thought that you have already arrived spiritually, you will not be able to continue in your reading, because we will be talking to you as if you are a fool. Now, I know that this will sound demeaning, but we have no other choice. You are not the lowliest beings, nor are you the most elevated ones, but somewhere in between. You are somewhere in the state of a fool. You cannot be pigeonholed. You cannot be ranked. As soon as you are, you tend to break those ties, those rankings. You cannot be free. You cannot be unfree. You cannot be free of self, but you cannot be tethered or constricted. You are the fool. God sees you as the fool, but also God sees you as an expression. This is not a bad view of you or even one which is condescending. It is one of loving insight. Abandon those things that you have taken with you in this life that tell you that you have arrived on some intellectual or spiritual level, because these will make an even greater fool out of you than the ordinary fool you are to begin with.

We hope you trust and understand that our intention is good and that we, ourselves, are beings of Light and Love here to translate something for you which is a lost part of your collective memory. And we hope that you receive it in the form in which it is given, knowing that in receiving it in this certain context, you are able to assimilate certain energy.

The Path is divided into two books. The first book consists of four parts that seem to be of travel and journeying. When you read Book One, you become a character who is journeying and making some kind of progress, or seeming to do something even if that something is only going inward. Book Two has five parts. These five parts represent states in which there is no need to journey, and no need to attain something. They represent, rather, states in which one functions on one's true level without preconceived ideas about who or what is journeying, whether the journey is being made, or whether the journey has an end. You know that all people on this Earth feel that they must get somewhere. You can appreciate that. You know that the social, political, and materialistic forces around you are designed to make you feel as if you must succeed. We, on the other hand, want you to abandon both success and failure. See yourself, not as someone who is journeying, but as someone whose ultimate purpose is to enjoy, to relish, to sit in, and to be in a state of fulfillment where you know that nothing is lacking. You know then you do not really have to go forward, or you do not have to go backwards. You are simply there, where your heart wishes you to be.

We have nothing good to say about those who wish to take your integrity away from you, who wish to violate your free will, who wish you to be subservient to their way of thinking. So we, in turn, are not in the slightest tempted to engage in this abrogation of God's agreement with you. We want you to read, not as one who needs to learn from the masters—although those beings whom you may call the masters are present in this book—but as one who accepts that we speak to you as friends. We speak to you, not bending down to your level, patronizingly— we speak to you because speech itself unites us, speech itself destroys all rankings and hierarchies. We speak to you as the One speaking to the many, or as the many speaking to each other, or as one of the many speaking to the many. We speak to you in love, and you are free to take or to leave what we have to give to you, or even to take or to leave the rather convoluted form in which it comes. You are free to take or to leave everything that is being said in its broad sense, or to take or to leave the particulars of what is being channeled to you. If you find one bit of insight to which you feel you can relate, even if it is only one, our purpose has been fulfilled. If you tend to resist this inclination because you are afraid of domination, please do not fret, for we are not beings with an agenda quite like that at all.

We ask you to sit back and to relax right now, having centered yourself. See how it feels to be in love. See how it is to feel joy in anticipation of what you are to receive. See how it feels to communicate on a higher level, because this is what you will be doing. Nature spirits, whom we call devas, angels, humans, animals, saints, even God Herself/Himself, will speak. You are here not just to listen or to receive. You are here as a participant. You cannot stop. If you force yourself to stop reacting to what you hear, then you will diminish the life force going through you that wishes you to be creative, to make use of what you have received, and to share. As we speak to you, we share with you and you share with us. Even though there is silence on your part, it is not total silence. You do not know all the ways in which you respond. You believe that verbal prayer to God is your only fitting response. We believe that your prayer is endless and takes on many forms.

My friends, I wish you Light and Love. I am the presenter of all the material that you will hear. And, I will come back at the end in Book 2, Part 5 to speak to you at length.

Now, God bless you and good-bye.

Book One

Part One
The Mountain

The First Ascent

We bring you greetings. I am a being of the world and a being who responds to what is not of this world, at the same time that I am of it. In the very recent past I walked this Earth as a princess. Would it be odd for me to come to you in written speech when you feel that you have so little connection with those members of royalty all over the world? How lowly your lives are! Or, how useless ours have been!

We trust that you have some understanding of self, enough to know that you, male and female, have been princes and princesses in your own hearts and minds. You know that your family has in many ways, for good or ill, treated you as princes or princesses. You have not led an idealized life, but no prince or princess has. There has been a potential to receive great authority and also an envy for it, even envy for this power that is to be yours coming from the king or the queen. You know that as majestic as a palace of a prince or princess may be, it is encumbered with customs and rules which dominate the lives of the royalty. We have not always been able to do exactly what we have wished to do, exactly that which needed to be accomplished to make us feel entirely free. We did not always know what to do to bring about happiness in our lives in such a repressive environment. But, on the other hand, we often felt that we had some freedom. And, we were able to accomplish much good in our position, even if it was a titular one.

So, I speak to you today as princesses and princes yourselves, because all of you have lived lives similar to this. All of you have gone through adolescence as princes and princesses. All of you have felt close to the reins of power, and yet have been unable to cross those last few inches with your hand and to grab those reins. All of you have felt that you have had demands upon you and have had few rewards for those demands. At the same time, you have felt that you have lived lives of privilege where you were able to acquire things with little or no work— homes, cars, food, clothing, entertainment, schooling—and have worried or troubled yourself in anticipation that perhaps you will not be able to sustain those blessings once you have reached adulthood. You see, our common ground is greater than our differences. So, it is most appropriate for you to be listening to me at this time. We start you on the journey, not as a common clod, a lowly being, but someone who is truly privileged, as you have been, to experience the riches of the world that are there simply because you are alive.

Our journey proper begins.

You have come of age in your small town. You find that you are walking along a street, with the cognizance that you have attained maturity in the body. You are no longer a child. You do not look up to the world, but look straight at it. You have some steadiness in your steps. You do not trip and fall or stumble as you often did in your childhood. You have some confidence in your stride. The realization that you have come of age has been a slow one, but you are now at the end of it. You have fulfilled the requirements of your society for the coming of age. You have been educated. You have been assimilated. You have been indoctrinated. Much has transpired. You have acquired a position of youth and promise. And this means that you now walk the street with great expectations of a life of fulfillment, the way lives have been described to you—material fulfillment, but also emotional fulfillment and perhaps even a hint of spiritual fulfillment.

As you walk the streets, before you and around you, spreads your town—the place which chose you to be alive, or the place in which you have chosen to be alive. Trees, squirrels and birds are about you. There are lawns, manicured and clean, with shrubbery and ornamental flowers, houses of various sizes and descriptions, filled with beings of various sizes and descriptions. There are the old, the young, the weak, the strong, the big and the small, some of one color, some of another, those who work with their hands, those who work with their minds, those who seem not to work at all. They come out of their houses; they greet you. It is a small town. They know you. And, in greeting you, they say, "Yes, my friend, you have come of age. You deserve to walk the streets secure in this knowledge."

Children play with their toys. Grown-ups take their vehicles and drive on the streets to destinations that are unknown to you, yet meaningful. All activity seems to have meaning, including your own. But, no one seems to reflect upon that meaning. Rather, they go about their tasks with a kind of euphoria.

As you continue, you pass more and more buildings. The sun is shining overhead. It is a clear day. A day, perhaps, of greater clarity than you normally experience. It is a warm day. A few clouds in the sky bring temporary relief from the burning sun but do not obscure its rays for long. You realize that everything is telling you that all is well. You are also realizing that, in walking, you are going toward the center of town, because the houses are dropping off and the businesses are starting to sprout up—a warehouse, a lumberyard, a gas station. You pass into the center of town. In the center there is a square you know, though you do not see it yet. Those business people in the center of town are even busier in their meaningful lives than those people who yet remain in their houses. From the big picture window the owner of the bookstore can be seen dusting books. The real estate agent is talking feverishly to someone. He is trying to close a deal. People are coming and going through the doors of the bank, as if they were the doors of a vault. They need a great effort to push themselves in to and to pull themselves out of this money chamber. Traffic is increased. The public is conveyed through a variety of means. You find that there are many other people walking on the sidewalk with you. Some are going in your direction, some are not. Some have an indolent pace, or some are hurried in their steps.

The closer you get to the town square, the greater the activity. Policemen come in and out of the police station. The bays of the fire station are open, and the engines are being cleaned. Someone at the fire station sits out on a chair watching, as if watching for small fires just in front of him. You see those places at which you most desire, now, to window-shop—clothing stores, food stores that have all your favorite treats. And you do. But, in continuing without being conscious of it, you have made your way to a certain place which is a park at the town square. You have arrived in your time at a park bench.

You know this place is your destination. But, as you sit on the bench, you immediately realize that you have forgotten how you have gotten there. In fact, your memory of self is quite strange. You know that you have arrived here, you know why, but somehow your origins seem to be unknown to you. There is a sudden shallowness in your memory, as if all of it has been just fabricated, and that you are a being invented yesterday.

Your true origins are foreign to you. You look out not as an alien, but as one who belongs and yet does not quite know themselves. You have arrived, but you have arrived to what? You have arrived from where? It lends a disquieting feeling to the day. Your mind does not remember its own birth, so how can it know where it is now if it does not remember from whence it has come?

You look around, and as you do, everything begins to take on a strange aspect. Something seems to be missing, or something seems to have been added. You are not sure which. Everything is in its place. There is not one person who is not doing their business and doing it appropriately. In fact, the whole world is aching with appropriateness. The vendors are selling their wares. The policemen are keeping watch. Children are playing in the park. The sky is blue overhead, as all skies should be. Nothing is misplaced. But there is something wrong, and you have a presage of some calamity.

What could be out of place in this most perfect world? You look up and see the sky. Surely the sky belongs up, blue and sunny. There is nothing wrong up there. The buildings all have roofs and windows; doors make ingress and egress possible. They are not at fault. The people are clothed in proper attire. They walk on two legs. They smile or they frown as you might expect, depending on what they are doing. They wince at labors when they strain under a heavy load, or they laugh like children playing with balloons. There is nothing wrong there. The leaves on the trees rustle. Squirrels jump from one branch to another. Birds sing. There is nothing before you that is amiss.

But then, as if you were again a small child, you look down along the path which stretches across the park. There is, for the moment, no intruding footstep. Beyond the sidewalk there is in front of you a long, lovely green lawn dotted with trees and shrubs. These are in place and all radiant with the summer light.

And, you see it. It is incredible that you have not seen it before, but it is there. On the ground there is a shadow—a shadow that casts itself almost as far as the eye can see, one big black shadow that stretches across the lawn in front of you. The shadow is a jagged triangle. The shadow has some foreboding to it or some promise, but you do not know what that is. You seek now, from your position on the bench, to find the source of the shadow. Some great object must be casting such a great shadow. You look around. "There is no one holding a cardboard triangle nearby," you say to yourself. "It would be moving if it were held by someone, or on some vehicle. But it is still. If it were alive like an animal or a tree, it would at least be shaking in the wind, and it is not. It must be fixed by human hands." You look at the buildings. The church has a peaked roof but the shadow is not darkness cast from the church. The church has its own shadow. The bank, the bakery, the fire station, city hall— no, it is none of these buildings.

Without realizing it, your vision goes skyward and you turn slightly to your rear, then you see it. It is a mountain. It is a great blue and snowy mountain. The mountain dominates the sky. You are shocked.

You have never seen this mountain before. You turn away from it. You see its shadow. You look again in back of you. You see the mountain looming even higher than it had before. It seems to be able to crush the town with its great weight. If a boulder fell from this mountain, it would roll into town, demolish houses and trees and crush people. "What is holding this mountain so close and intact? Why have I never noticed the mountain before?"

You are surprised. You are alarmed, but intensely curious. "I have been educated in this town for these many years, and no one has spoken of the mountain before. Is the mountain a taboo subject?" You question yourself over and over, but you cannot arrive at an answer. You say to yourself, "I must find out what this mountain means and why I have not seen it before." You stand up and start to walk.

The nearest person happens to be a policeman who is walking towards you, smiling. You are not, after all, a criminal. He knows you. "Good day," he says. "Good day," you say. Not wanting to speak of the mountain directly, you engage in some light conversation and then you insert a question. "The mountain is looking magnificent, is it not, today in the sunlight?" The policeman looks at you as if you are crazy and looks into the direction you have just indicated where you can see, as plain as day, a mountain of immense size and portent. He turns back to you and he says, "Are you feeling ill?" "No," you say. "Then you are pulling my leg, for there is no mountain there." He laughs and, as he goes, says, "There are no mountains in this part of the world. You need a better joke than that." You are dumbfounded.

Next, you come across an old lady. Though you do not know her, she appears very maternal, very kindly. "Good day, ma'am." "Good day," she says to you. "Do you see?" you ask. "I believe some birds have flown off the mountain and are coming into town. Are they on a migratory route?" She looks at you in revulsion. "Mountain? In a faraway place there are mountains, but how would you know if the birds came from there?" "No," you say, "it is this mountain right here that forms the valley in which the town is nestled." She looks at you intensely as if you are meaning harm to her. She steps away to your side and goes on without saying a word. She could not see the mountain either.

Surely, you believe, innocent children whose eyes are not closed from years of adult life will give you a straight answer. So next, you come across a small child. "Hello, little girl," you say, "It is a beautiful day." "Yes," she nods her head, "I'm having fun." She indicates that she wants to move on. "By the way, have you ever drawn a picture of the mountain?" And you point to the mountain. She looks in the direction you are pointing and says that you are very silly. "There's nothing there." And she moves on.

You are very distressed. You know that you must stop asking these questions, because it is obvious that no one else can see the mountain. Your elders would have shown it to you before, and they did not. It has not just arrived from out of town, or else it would have created a big stir, would it not? You look again. Are you deluding yourself? Delusion is not a habit of your mind. No, it is there. You are firm in this, for after all, you have achieved something in this world. Perhaps, because you have, you know that what is in front of you is real. It is too grand and too solid not to be. It must be that others live in an illusory world, and that is the reason why they cannot see it. It must be that it holds something very frightening for them.

You reposition yourself on another bench. Before you, everyone continues to go about their prosaic tasks. It seems to be a sane world. Maybe it is a too-sane world, too sane to acknowledge such an incomprehensible presence around it. Maybe the mountain threatens, and those around you that cannot see it refuse to out of fear. But, more than ever now, you ache with a desire to know what this mountain is and what it represents. You thirst to experience it, and you do not know why. You search for a way in. The humans around you are ignorant. The thought occurs to you that perhaps an animal can best serve you at this point. You propose to inwardly seek this kind of guidance and it now comes to you.

At this point, my friends, I will depart and allow you in love to experience the next ascent.

God bless you all.

The Dog

⬣ # The Second Ascent

Y ou are here because you want to know. You seek out somebody who knows, or seems to know, or seems to be playing in knowledge. And I come to you.

I am of the animal kingdom. I am, in fact, a dog. Whose dog, you do not know. I am a dog in the park. The dog in the park knows everything, or else the dog in the park has not the confidence to engage in such silly play. The dog must hold something. You poor miserable person, I come to you now. I run around your legs. I am trying to engage you in play. It is a common thing, but in the context of your conundrum, I have come to rescue you. I am here to save you—man's best friend. I am just a small dog, a little terrier, but I do know a few things. And you can tell by the smile on my face and my willingness to play with you that I hold some knowledge in me. "Why not seek out the wisdom of the animals," you say, "since humans have failed me?" And I hold such wisdom, as I said.

Dogs play with sticks. You pick up a stick and you throw it in the direction of the mountain. I chase after it and bring it back. I know what you are up to, for I see the mountain myself. You throw it again in the direction of the mountain. Again I bring it back. Again you throw it, and again I bring it back. I am telling you that I know the mountain is there, even though I am not willing or able to speak it.

At a certain point, I stop our play because, even for a dog, catching sticks can get boring. I bark and I start to run off. I stop. I turn around and I bark at you again. And I run off again. I am asking you to follow.

"What good times we can have together," I am saying. You are saying, "Will you lead me to this mountain?" I am saying, "This is where all the good times are. Follow me." And you do. Who is throwing the stick now, and who is fetching? We have traded places.

I lead you across the small park through the concrete ruts between buildings, bit by bit, out of town. Here, there is a broad field. And this field you have seen before, but never in this context. Perhaps some sport was played here or some festival was held here. I am more than pleased that you are willing to follow me. I am content that you are willing to share with me the splendor of the day and the awareness of the mountain. Pleased as you are that I bring something of that mountain with me, here in this field, you think we can again engage in play. You pick up another stick and you throw it in the direction of the mountain. As I snatch it up again, you now know for certain where this conversation is heading. It is heading toward a discussion of the mountain.

The field you are in provides the wind with many privileges to maneuver, a greater ease to move in a flow. The wind is coming from the mountain. You feel it coming from that direction. As I bring back a stick, I stop and I smell your pants at the ankle and I look up to you. And you realize that you are to smell the breeze which is coming from the mountain. As you face it and close your eyes, then look up and take a deep breath, I sit and look up and take a deep breath myself. There is nothing like the air that comes from a place which remains cold through the summer. There is nothing as refreshing as the air which has caressed its impenetrable surface, taking with it the moisture of ice and snow. It is a wonderful thing in itself just to smell it. This is your knowledge right now, the knowledge that the mountain can be experienced from a distance, that it can be felt and known from a distance.

I will soon depart. I have my people. Perhaps you have people to whom you need to go at some time, although not now. As we both stare ahead, we see a form coming from the distance on high. It is a bird. This bird moves with much assuredness through the air. Our eyes now are focused on it. It has left the mountain and is coming in our direction. And it is from here that I must depart.

Good-bye, my friend. I am going home and getting some refreshments—table scraps. I leave you with your next guide.

◭ The Third Ascent

A ll of your life, so far, things have come to you one step at a time. You have worked towards certain ends and found those ends fulfilled. The business of the world seems to rise and fall upon effort applied in the right manner with the right intention and the right goal in mind. But, as I come to you carried by the wind which flows down the mountainside into your small town, you realize that not everything is acquired through great effort. There are some things that simply fly in the wind with ease and grace. As my image becomes larger and larger in your eyes, you are better able to discern my shape and size, and who I am.

I am a falcon. I am a falcon that has perched upon the mountain and surveyed your world from that vantage point. And I come to you bringing you something of the mountain, a souvenir. As I grow larger and larger you become excited and apprehensive. You realize that the dog has left you and that I am to be your next messenger. I fly overhead, closer and closer. I show much elegance and joy in flight. I am not stifled by your world, and I cannot be brought down by it. I have a transcendent presence. It is a presence of strength, courage and grace. As I come closer, I cry out, and you hear my shriek and inwardly rejoice. Then, as I swoop overhead, something happens.

It must have been that I held something in my claws, and I chose this time to release it, because down to the ground from just above you, there falls a twig. It is right before you. You see it and you pick it up. The twig has some pine needles on it. You look toward the mountain from where the twig has come. And you look above. Truly, I am a herald of this mountain come to entice you on a journey to it. You touch the twig. You have seen the mountain. You have smelled the mountain. And now, you have touched the mountain. What a magnificent place it is. What a great ambition it would be to climb the mountain, or at least, to approach it, to lie at its foothills and to look up at its magnificence. Surely, this could be a purpose worthy of a human: to approach the mountain, to conquer it with your understanding. Surely, you will be able to carry this experience with you throughout your life.

You will bear something away from this mountain in the manner in which I have carried with me this twig. You hold onto it as if it is a promise from God. You look above at me again. I am circling above you, around and around. I am giving you my blessings, or so it seems. I am blessing you, and I am flying back again. Will you follow? That seems to be the question I ask. In truth, I do not know you, but I have been sent from this mountain, and I need you to receive something, as much as you need to receive something. It was our way of talking, to have dropped this twig before you. It was our way of communicating. This token is better than words, better than predigested thoughts. There are flowers in the field, swaying to the breeze which carries me back. Color, now, seems to have been excited and calls out in anticipation of a quest. The mountain seems to have grown in size and magnificence. You are going to break from your old path and cut out a new one, carried along by the sensation of the mountain. You are going towards it, and you know it. You know that you must.

At this time, the vast countryside in front of you daunts your desire to go forward, and you realize that you need to seek out some guide. You turn and head back towards town. You desire to get provisions together for a long journey and to find some help to get you through the terrain in order to properly begin your ascent.

So, I leave you to your tasks. And, perhaps, I will see you at some appointed place in the future, where you will be closer to my home, my nest.

We wish you Light and Love.

The Old Guide

◬ The Fourth Ascent

You seek me out, for the first time. Others have sought you out before this, but now, for the first time, you have sought out someone yourself. I am that human being. What a strange way for us to meet. We are here as a guide but also as a master. We are your first master, your first true teacher. And we are privileged and happy to be this.

Thus far, you have not determined the scope of your education. Now, you have taken control of it, and have sought me out. I abide in the small town in which you live. For the first time you come to me having heard that I am good at traveling and that I am also a good guide in this respect - to set other travelers on their journey. We talk about how much time you need to get to your destination. We talk about how you must prepare yourself, or what you can expect.

I do not speak to you of the mountain. Is it that I do not know it? Or, is it that I just will not speak of it? You are not sure at this time. You are confident in your direction and really do not need to engage me in dialogue about the mountain. But, you have had enough disappointments in communication and in finding common ground in perception, as far as this is concerned, to cause you hesitate to engage me in discussion of it. Indeed, the fact of the matter is that I do not see the mountain at all.

You hire your first teacher, and I set out with you the next morning on this journey. The purpose of this journey I do not know. I am simply your guide and your teacher. It does not matter to me what the end of your journey ultimately is. Indeed, there may be things that I see about which you would have no idea. So, it is possible that I am simply respecting your privacy and your willingness and desire to hold an ideal close to you. I will not fiddle around with it; I will not contaminate it. It could be that I have deep respect for you and your inner vision. However, you see the mountain as beyond yourself. It is quite possible that it is, but, you can only engage me while I treat you as if this mountain is an inner goal. So we set off.

The breadth of my knowledge is apparent. I know the dialects of the people whom we will meet. I know how the countryside is laid out. I know to walk during the day and sleep at night, and that sometimes it rains and the traveling is more difficult; sometimes we need to stay on the road and sometimes we need to leave it. I know all these things, but I also know the fine details. I know the wild berries and plants we can eat, and flowers we can pick along the way. I know which roots to pull up from the ground and make part of our lunch. I know the ways of the animals: who to avoid and when, where to find a nest, perhaps, that has a few savory eggs. I know the ways of the peoples in this mountain valley. I know their habits and customs. I understand what will offend them and what will please them. I speak enough in their manner to know.

You see, everyone comes from a small place and journeys to a grander one. Everyone seeks broadening and seeks to free themselves from their own narrow past. It is really on this basis that I relate to all those around me.

I know this land, and it will take us quite some time to get to your goal. We are climbing higher and higher, step by step, but I do not seem to notice. Sometimes it seems to you that the terrain is getting slightly rockier. We are passing fewer and fewer towns. Our means of locomotion—our own two legs—carries us rather slowly. But, on the other hand, it seems most appropriate to you to be traveling in this way, as it gives me time to help you adjust to traveling itself, and to impart to you some of the basic knowledge that I have about everything we are doing. And, it appears as if you cannot take in everything that you must take in to achieve your goal. You must hold on to some reserve of energy and not just catapult yourself into the foothills of this mountain. You must become accustomed to the journey and tolerant of its pitfalls and necessities.

I talk and I talk, perhaps too much. At some time in our journey you start to become vexed. It seemed as if at first I had an abundance of information with me, but my lack of recognition of that mountain is annoying you. And, my words, as we travel these days and weeks, become more and more like babbling. I seem to skirt around the issue more and more. I seem to be unable to get to the point.

You are starting to become annoyed. This is my tactic, but you do not see it. I love and respect that which you hold in your heart and the vision of your ideals being attained, but I cannot tell you this without violating you. So, I deliberately choose to go on endlessly until you see that it is time for us to part. With sadness, but with resolve, you try to make the separation.

You are now very close to the foothills of the mountain. The mountain has been getting larger and larger, of course, all the time. It is hard to miss once you have set your mind on it. And now you have the confidence that you can find your way alone in these last days. You find some excuse to tell me to go away. You say that the journey is nearly ended and you need to be alone, which is true. However, I do not respond immediately to these remarks. I wait. You say, in so many words, that you are tired of my company, that we need to part for the sake of our own peace of mind. I can accept that. Or, you say that you need to go on to greater guidance. And this I have known all along.

In any event, some words are exchanged peacefully, but with some hurt feelings. Finally I depart. I will simply go back, because I have not been interested in journeying except to help you. And, I know, my friend, that you will go on.

There are many of us in the world who are your guides for a time, your teachers or masters, whom you believe can impart to you great wisdom. But we are ignorant of that which you hold inside and, ultimately, that which you see before you in life. Please hear that we mean no harm. We are here to serve you in love and in peace.

We bid you adieu.

The Messenger Angel

◭ The Fifth Ascent

We greet you as friends and in the spirit of friendship we share what we can. I am of the angelic kingdom, and I bring you messages from those who otherwise cannot speak for themselves. So, now, as you are at the foothills of this mountain, you hear a message. As you face the mountain, the sun shines from behind it in great brilliance, highlighting its white cap. You hear the message, borne on the angel's wings. And I am that angel, a messenger angel, come to you to bring a greeting from the very peak of the mountain. You must have heard the message before. In fact, you have unconsciously heard it. It has been a subliminal communication, but a very powerful one. The dog has given you the smell of the mountain. The falcon has given you its touch. The old man has opened your eyes. You have seen this mountain, but you have not heard it, or you have been unwilling to acknowledge your hearing of it. But, now, you become conscious. Facing the mountain you are conscious of the potency of its sound. It has a profound sound, a sound resonant in the lowest vibrations. Your hearing is being affected by it. But, also, it vibrates the soles of your feet. It is like a tremor of the Earth herself. The sound of this mountain is the sound of its own birth. It was born to this sound, to a great trembling of the Earth. The splitting of the Earth's crust was the creation of the mountain's unique voice.

When you stand in this ultimate confrontation, you bring forth the awareness needed to attain the heights. This final preparation for your ascent will bring to your consciousness whatever you have hidden, even from yourself. This sound which shakes the Earth and causes things to topple over or to crumble—the sound like the forming of a great mountain— has been shaking the roots of your self-knowledge, has been shaking all of your preconceived ideas. The ground, too, has been shaking your willingness to continue by moving underneath your feet. It has been shaking everything imaginable that is important until you see that the rupture which has brought this mountain into being is the only thing important to you now.

We speak for the many who otherwise cannot speak. We are a messenger angel much like those you have heard many times deliver messages of birth or of death or of the next life. It is our pleasure, but also our duty, to give you this message. Too much has been stilled inside you, and your attention has wandered at the same time. Now that you are uneasy, unsettled, and ambitious, what is outside you has remained still. The mountain now has curtailed its upheaval. No longer does it erupt from the Earth. It sings the memory of its own birth. This is now imparted to you and becomes a quaking inside you. You are that mountain forming. You are one with it before you have even set one foot properly on a single stone. You are one with the experience of its pinnacle. You have been there in some way, and you are going to return now.

The mountain, in toning, does not give its name, but shares its essence with you. Its name is the secret which will be disclosed to you after your ascent. And, this you know. More than ever, this unnamed, unknown mountain calls to you in a profound way. More than ever you hear and hear again its cry, the cry of its own birth, but the cry of its need to call to you. This is the siren's call. "You will hear my name when you reach my peak. You will know me when you are with me in body." It is inevitable that you continue.

My friends, we have nothing more to share. We cannot make your footsteps fall more quickly or more firmly. We cannot motivate you. We step back from our activity so that the messenger is unattached to the outcome or even to the message being received at all. You can assume that our message is complete as far as it could be, or you can question yourself and hope that there is more to it than what you have heard. This will not be the case. We have given up everything. All learning needed to continue has been laid at your feet. We are hopeful that you will heed all this as a good omen. The sound of the mountain is a good omen for you, but where it will take you, no one knows, least of all yourself.

We thank you.

The Bear

◭ # The Sixth Ascent

I am the spirit of the bears. We speak for all of us to you as an individual.

Your footsteps now seem almost hastened by this last communication. You are joyful in anticipation and energized by both the message and the messenger herself. We acknowledge this joy. We show you with our hulking bodies what it is like to move in joy and solitude, for bears are solitary animals. We show you what it is like now as you move forward to apply force to its greatest extent. As the trees clear and you see outcroppings of rock, you witness us in our solitary play. One bear after another seems to be showing you how your path must be one of great strength, one of great purposeful effort, one of great joy in anticipation. We climb rocks better than you can imagine. We are here to teach but we cannot act as your guide. For all guides must accompany you and bind themselves in some way to you. We will not bind ourselves to any other. But, in our way, we are the best teachers, because at this point in your journey you must go it alone. You need only to be shown that it is possible to do so, to climb the heights by yourself, to achieve the pinnacle as a lone being.

You are refreshed and encouraged by watching us. Invigorated, your steps become more assured. You move from rock to rock as the mountain sweeps upward. Your climb becomes more perilous. Now, hands must accompany feet in getting you to reach the peak. Now, hands must find one hold after another, and the feet must complement them. Step by step now becomes handhold by handhold. Your breathing becomes more deliberate. You fill up your lungs with air as if each inhalation was something precious. You are seeing that the way of the bear is one of great solitary effort. It is one of relentless force, and yet it is peaceful in the extreme. There is nothing that you are disturbing or harming. You need only to take in what you need to live. It is the bear that takes only what it needs to live. We do not play with our food. We do not seek to torment our prey. We do not engage in conflict for no reason. We, instead, live solitary, peaceful lives enjoying the fruits of the land, the comforts of the body. We are also equally capable of strenuous effort. This is you, now.

It is time for you to look at the peak and to focus your attention on it. It is now that you know that good effort is its own reward, that mindful effort is a great gift. This is what you have. Are you proud?

Yes, you are. Pride is swelling up inside of you. Maybe it is spilling over the rocks as you grab on to them. Each handhold and each foothold seems to be another step up a monumental pyramid, another step up an undetermined hierarchy. You are lavishing achievement on yourself, and it is creating a great being, a being willing to put so much effort and endurance into the climb. Endurance is needed, for your physical ascent has just begun.

Without knowing it, you have passed us. You have reached a point where you need to look downward to see us. And in the end, you are no longer content to do so. A downward gaze prevents you from keeping your mind on the goal. So it is that we are no longer symbols to you of that courage and strength of spirit which you have inside. We become ghostly, and you seek a new focus.

Eventually, you begin to gaze at the peak of the mountain itself. Because it is high above you, it also means that right in front of you is a very sheer wall of rock. There is nothing much there to see. If you want to examine the small crevices, they will not be found full of life. There is nothing great lurking in them. The rock face is now forcing you to gaze upward. There an intense sun illuminates the snowy peak. It is yours if you will take it.

You will yourself at the next stage of your journey. And, it is here, my friends, that we, the bears, depart.

The North Wind Deva

◬ The Seventh Ascent

I bring you greetings, not from the animal realm, or from the realm of humans, or even the realm of flora. I am the spirit of the north wind. We are here with you. We come to impart our wisdom to you.

You have made one firm foothold, have reached out and made one firm handhold, again and again. Hold by hold, you are ascending the mountain, climbing the rock face, its final aspect. Below you are the bears. They have left you, and you can no longer emulate them because they are no longer in your vision. The birds have gone to their perches; they remain unseen by you in the mists and snow. Indeed, nothing that you would call alive, except for the rock itself, is with you. You are truly alone, truly solitary and working at your limit.

At this time, when your activity is so rarified, my energy comes to you, the force of the wind which blows from the north. We blow from the north as if from the crown of the planet. We blow from the north like messengers of some higher state of being. We blow cold and chilling, but we blow sweet and clear like the ether. We accompany you on your journey at this point. We are your guides. We bring to you now the strength necessary to continue. You can no longer sustain yourself with bearlike energy, for your intake of breath is becoming more labored, as the air is thinner. You can no longer operate like some large animal. The thinness of the air is like that of your life itself. You see yourself as someone whose existence dangles from the mountainside. You see yourself as someone who must make the best out of the little nourishment that you now receive. It is the least that you have ever received from the Earth.

We give you energy, as we say. We bring you the force of nature itself, and we impart to you some energy that is ours and is the only thing which we can share, for we do not speak and we cannot hear. The chilling sweetness of the north wind is like an elixir. It is like a frosty drink. Each intake of breath shared in the north wind becomes like drinking a draft of this clear elixir. We blow down the side of the mountain and curl back up through the valley and blow again up its stony face. We can fill you like a sail, but the power is from those most rarified heights.

You are climbing even beyond your imagination, climbing to a point which you can no longer see, a point so vertical, a pinnacle so steep you cannot see its end. A focus point is best for keeping your mind on the goal and keeping yourself in forward motion. But, it is impossible to see your goal. The sun shines like the only star and blots out your vision of the summit, which you crave to reach.

So, we are here to tell you that the energy which we bring, so precious, so jewel-like, so elegant, is enough to sustain you the rest of the way. We do not bring you hope. We do not bring you faith. We bring you an elevated joy and sense of purpose. Through our instruction you press onward to the noblest and the highest. It is as if you are, by ingesting this elixir, not becoming one with the mountain, but one with its breath.

You have become one with us, and as a comrade, we bear you along. You do not know what it will take to get you to your destination. It seems as if the vitality that is coming through you is not of this Earth, it is so etheric. But, it is energy which is palpable. It shoots through your being like lightning through a rod. Feet and hands work in concert and bring you to new elevations.

You look down for one last time. No longer can you clearly see the valley floor. The trees have become like small green balls. The wildlife is beyond your vision. You look up. You are truly alone. You are truly one in this solitary experience. There will be no one to save you if you fall. You do not depend upon us, but we join forces with you. You do not lean against the mountainside either; you use it to push against. And this is what is guiding you, the wind and the rock face. Soon you realize that your destination is at hand, and the steps needed to reach it are few. The elixir has made you intoxicated, and you are almost becoming dizzy and giddy with excitement. No matter how much you believe you have labored and suffered to get to where you are, it seems that this is all worthwhile. The heart beating in the chest, the lungs expanding and contracting in a way they have never done before, is just verification of the legitimacy of your climb. Surely, there is something great and noble awaiting you at the peak.

We thank you.

PART TWO
The No Place

The No Place

Your journey is almost complete. There only remain a few more handholds and a little more exertion to reach the top, and you know it. These last few efforts are thrilling. What has happened is that, at last, the sensory world has been shucked. Through one sense after another and beyond each sense, you have abandoned your home. You have climbed up this mountain, and then the wind deva has given you that last impulse which is of mind and goes beyond all senses. This is what is now, in these last few handholds, leading to your rightful place on the mountaintop.

The material world is far below your feet. The sensory world has left with it. The air, so pure, so rarified, is an exhilarating sensation. As much as you believe that you can feel pain in your exertion, you now know that the mind can allow you at once to feel joy. You choose the mind, and you choose joy. Reaching the final rock ledge, one hand follows the other, one foot follows the other, and then, from your crouching position, you slowly stand erect. With shoulders back and head high, you look about. The sun which had been on the other side of the mountain is now crystalline and radiant. It is the most brilliant sun that you have ever seen. There is nothing in the least bit to obscure it. Below you from where you have come, all the details of the world are condensed into one brief valley across the length of which you believe that you could cast a small pebble. The prosaic world has been cast down at your feet. As you have ascended, it has fallen below you. You are truly at the heights. You rejoice, because you believe that all of your effort has gotten you a fine reward. Truly there must be a God. And, truly this is the sight and sense of God. This mountain peak upon which you stand must be the vision of God. You know that this is your great achievement.

My friends, I speak to you from the realm of the angels. I am the Archangel Michael and, perhaps, it was I who placed the mountain at your feet. Upon it now you stand assured of self, of your accomplishment, and of your purpose. You spin around ecstatically. The world has indeed been laid at your feet. Untold numbers of beings are beneath you. They have been surpassed by you and seem insignificant. It is even that your personal history has been obscured by your achievement; such is its divine nature. No longer alone, you have attained heaven; you are in communion with God. A potent drug courses through your system. It is injected by your self-deliverance to the peak and elevates you alone to this direct communication with the God of the natural world. Everything in your ecstasy is telling you that you are one with this God. Again you spin, head raised to the sky, arms outstretched, hands free and empty.

And then, almost as if you have taken a breath too many, or that you realize that the source of your strength has been mere impulse, a certain anxiety comes over you. It seems to come out of the blue sky or from nowhere. Maybe it comes from some stratospheric place which the sun will not allow you to penetrate with the eyes alone. Realization is dawning upon you. You look down at your feet and see that, as huge as this mountain is and as much labor that you have put into conquering it, you do not understand it. If you are standing on the peak of this mountain and you are addressing God, then God is in the heavens and with your face pushed up against the vault of the heavens, you can speak to God, but the mountain has yet to reveal itself to you.

You knew that you must come here. You knew inherently that you needed to understand it. But the mountain has yet to disclose itself to you. You may have conquered it, but you do not know it. You are standing on it. It is supporting you and, yet, you are in disbelief of it. You are the fool on the precipice. The mountain has not spoken to you in words which you could comprehend or perhaps, it has not spoken to you at all. Which is it?

You look around for a clue. There is the blue sky that is unimaginably transparent and vacant. There is the burning sun that is stark, passionate, but unyielding. Below you there are the green clumps

The No Place

that form the trees on the hills in the valley. But there is nothing discernible which can guide you there. Without your awareness of it, clouds are forming around the mountain like dandelion seed heads. They collect along its broad sides as in dance. They move in a secret narrative. They come to curtail your vision and your sense of place, even the sense of the great height that you have climbed.

As they do, your perch seems more vertiginous. You sense that something is being said to you. For all your journey, you have not truly wondered what the mountain was. Your wonderment was that it was there at all. Your understanding of it was not enhanced by your tenacity to climb it. As you drew closer, it had been, in reality, pulling farther away from you. Its meaning has been eluding you.

But now, the clouds gathering beneath are starting to summon some understanding to you. You realize that something is causing fear and, yet, is a thought and a sensation which must be explored. Now that the clouds have gathered completely around the mountain, you do not see the valley anymore. You cannot locate your point of origin. You have no reference left. Soon you become aware that perhaps the clouds are not simply encircling the mountain, but are eating away at it and undermining its foundation. The mountain will no longer be there. The wind sweeps the clouds upward towards you. Your vision is getting as obscured as the clouds themselves. The mountain is vaporizing.

And then, a chill comes across you as you awake to what the mountain has been, and what it always has been, and what your achievement has been, and what your purpose has been in getting there. You understand what you have so longed to know, and you are frightening yourself by what you realize have been your desires. You have come to see emptiness itself. The mountain is that emptiness which has set itself there and continues there through all of life. It is complete emptiness. Through this emptiness the clouds are showing you that a mountain can be swept away. You appeal to it almost in a scream; your mind cries out like that of a child. You appeal to it to stay where it is, but it will not do this. You cannot remake the mountain because it has not been made by you. Perhaps this would have saved you, but this is not the case. What has made emptiness, you do not know. But you do know that you have maneuvered your person so that you now stand on top of a vast emptiness which has swelled from the bowels of the Earth and crested up into the shape of a mountain. You are alone on top of it, in a Godless place.

Your pride in achievement was as empty as the mountain. Your ambitions were as cold-driven as the wind that pushes the clouds. You are facing what you most need to confront and what is the most fearful for you now. Where is your vision of God? You do not have it but you call for it. Why did the pursuit of emptiness call to you, instead? Where is God?

My friends, deep within you, you search. In your searching, you hope to find, and in your finding, you hope to know. But there is nothing in the universe that comes to you in order. If you search for God, you will not find Him. If you attempt to achieve, you will only find in the pinnacle of your success that you are bereft of God. We can ask you: have you been attempting to find God in this journey? You have ostensibly been attempting to understand the mountain. The mountain has revealed itself to be emptiness. Have you been searching for God? You think now, standing on that tiny ledge, that you have been, without knowing it.

You comprehend that in walking the streets of your town, having the feeling that you had arrived, and trying to walk in the knowledge of self, you had instead been discontent and so have taken this journey to find peace of heart through knowledge. With all this great effort you have put forth, you have found only emptiness. And this emptiness begins to eat at you, as the clouds gnaw at the side of the mountain. If it is God whom you have been pursuing, why did you not confess it? If it was self-knowledge that you sought, why did you not remain still? You have been on a fool's journey, or so you think. You cannot call out to the emptiness, because your words are swallowed up in it. They return no wisdom to you. In fact, as the mountain seems to be taken away, and as all your gifts and all your achievements are shown to be vacant, you think only of rescue and safety.

Your state of mind, now, is not a heightened one. It is one of base survival. If you do not leave, the emptiness will eat you. You will be swallowed up in emptiness. You feel it and you know it. You realize with a thud and a shudder that you have been on a fool's errand, and so now you must turn from this. If you turn to something which you have not yet seen, it will be what is on the other side of the mountain, which could be clearly visible to you, but which you have not yet witnessed. In silence you cry out, "If there is a God, I will find some way to be delivered from this emptiness." And you wait.

The messenger arrives before your flesh becomes brittle from the cold and your lungs exhausted from the lack of vital air. You cast down your eyes to the other side of the mountain for the first time. And, it is there that you obtain your next guidance.

My friends, I wish you to realize that it is possible for you to achieve great things in this world and to find that they bring you nothing but emptiness. If you do not desist from this fool's journey, you will be an even greater fool. And, if you do not comprehend that this journey has been such a fool's journey, you will never achieve wisdom. Whatever you have searched for has been meaningless, because in searching for it you have found only emptiness. In trying to reach a goal, no matter how visible the goal seems to be, or how noble, or how enticing the goal seems, you will always end up in emptiness. Turn now to the task at hand. You need to deliver yourself from your own folly. You are willing to make an effort to save yourself. It is only you who has gotten yourself to this point. It is truly only you who can save yourself. You realize this. You must continue, but now your searching is over. If you go forward in this life, you will go forward in exploration, but not as a conqueror, for that is a fool's journey, not as someone seeking, for that will also deliver you into emptiness, but as someone willing to experience and explore. This is your determination and your will. Your will is now peaking with as great a strength of force as the mountain. The mountainous peak, in fact, is nothing compared to your will, which you realize has sustained you all this time and will continue to sustain you, because it now shows itself to be greater than this emptiness, greater than each and every rock formation of the mountain. Your will is driving you into the Light. You look towards the sun that begins now to set, and you see that your will can sustain you and deliver you from emptiness.

At this point, my friends, we must leave and give you to another. We have no answers for you at this stage, although it may appear to you that we are holding answers deep within us and are selfishly guarding them, unwilling to share. But, a fool does not receive wisdom, nor can he give it, anyway. If you are now looking to me for answers, I will turn my head from you. We have stood with you on this peak without your knowing it. And, we have helped you to realize what has been motivating you has been your own sense of being, your will to live, but not your ability to think - not your cunning, but your instinct. What could sustain you on such a foolish search? Not your intellect, but your desire for life. And now you own this desire and you realize that the emptiness is helping you understand. This will to live can guide you into wisdom much better than anything else.

And so I leave you now in the care of another. We see that you have unconsciously made your journey in love; this has been the only honor that you have bestowed upon yourself. It is a secret honor, and you have held it secret for quite some time. But now, I confess to you that I have seen it all along. There is love in your willingness to live. And, in the foolishness in taking up the trek, there has always been love. As we have said, this has bestowed the greatest honor upon you. This is the most honorable thing that you have achieved.

Good-bye.

Part Three

The Lake

● The First Descent

My friend, you must know now that it is time for you to descend. You can feel it in your bones.

You have become more anxious. It is more critical than ever for you to receive the force which drives your will to survive. The message that you receive from this life force within you is without blandishments; to live, you must get off the mountain. You are not moved by fear, but by a desire to live. And you are at peace with this. As much as you could allow fear to overwhelm you, you have the courage to maintain your composure and to allow that life force within you to motivate your physical body and your mental body into a cooperative effort of descent. So, you begin to release yourself from that emptiness of the mountain. You begin a downward climb.

You have looked around and determined that it is impossible to return to where you have been. And, although you were not able to study the landscape to the horizon, you make an instinctive decision, which is really a decision from a higher plane, to descend the other side of the mountain and explore what is down there. But you are now weary from the long climb upwards and your steps are not as sure as they had been in the ascent. You scrape your skin on the rocks and your hands begin to bleed. There is enough will for you to continue, but there is not enough strength in your soul for you to continue in joy or in confidence.

Now, descending the steep slope of the mountain and struggling to maintain your equilibrium while you are gasping for air, you seek some sign of hope, something to awaken inner faith in you. You seek some outward sign of God's grace and mercy for the fool who is now climbing off his precarious pedestal. You look below you. And, although as taxing as this is to see yourself aloft on such a height, ungrounded and disconnected from all the living, while you get the opportunity, you stare, searching for this sign.

The wind does not blow in any familiar way. It is neither rising up the side of the mountain nor cascading down it. It is not blowing into it or wrapping itself around it like a blanket. The wind is now coming up in puffs and gusts. The cloud formations here are light, but resilient to the wind. They cluster about, beneath you.

The wind seems to be playing with you now. You might think that mockery is the response to your soul's outcry. But this is not the case. This temptation passes quickly, in any event, because you realize that, as you are working your way down, the wind becomes a calling to you to awaken to something new. Faith in God, the God that you have yet to acknowledge, is possible without belief in God. You begin to comprehend that you have called to God because you have desired to continue living. Your will has called out to God as much as one's heart can call out to God. Your desire to live has called out; the call has been returned, and you have heard it returned.

The wind is beginning to pantomime your call. In the light of the setting sun, something catches your eye. It is impossible, you think, for what you see to be real. And yet, it is impossible that you see it and it not be so, for the air is too cold and the strain on your body, in the effort which you are putting forth, is too painful for you to be dreaming.

What do you see but a butterfly far below you, plainly discernible? You see that the butterfly plays as if it is the wind itself flickering around the side of the mountain, the wind, which has no direction, the wind which seems to be all play and no effort. The butterfly in red, gold, and black is the most beautiful thing that you have ever seen. You drink its vision in. It is vital and vibrant in the place in which you labor in so much anxiety. It is alive and playing in a place that is so inhospitable to you.

And then there is a pause. The butterfly passes down into a cloud. You think, perhaps, that it is leaving you to tell you that to be alive it must be someplace else. But this is just a passing thought. You see that it has a different purpose. It does, in fact, return. Coming through and flickering above the cloud now, it has brought with it its

The First Descent

many friends. There are now one, two, three, four, five, six butterflies. You are counting them and, as you count them, you seem to be creating them, or seem to be summoning them into existence. Seven, eight, nine, ten— they become uncountable. In this small miracle they join with you in a way you do not yet understand. But this vision has inspired faith. The last thing you saw which was alive on the mountain was a great bear. The last things you wanted to think could survive in this place were the most delicate and beautiful creatures. And yet they are here. It must be faith itself that keeps them alive in a place where only the bear is at home. It must be faith that motivates them to ascend and to dive down through the clouds again, and then to pull themselves up and circle each other playfully. It must be faith that lets them know they will be fed and nourished in the place to which they go. It must be faith that enables them to continue their race in this harsh climate.

You are, at this time, descending and becoming more at ease with the descent, because of the vision which my beings have given you. I am the deva of the butterfly. I am here to share with you. Like a faint, flickering candle, we light the way. We are not above you nor below you, but we are with you in heart. Do you know the place that you hold within, which you do not or will not show to others—that place where the burning candle flickers and shines— which you will not describe to another for fear it will be violated, for fear of its delicacy? We are that place, externalized. What is it but your soul? It is that which you have so long believed could not exist, the thought of which the practical world has told you to squelch, one which a remote and uncaring God has not allowed you to appreciate. But, if we, the small and the weak, could fly with abandoned delight in this world, then so also can you ignite and keep lit that light of the soul that is you. You know that this must be the case, for we say this to you with every flutter of our wings.

You have no time to absorb the significance of what we symbolize for you, for all effort is made to join mind and body. But, what you can grasp gives you the faith to continue. And you do. At this point we are, in our freedom of movement, enabling each other to go forward in joy, for we see you also, and we rejoice that your life has not been extinguished, that your soul light is still flickering.

So, follow us. What better guide do you need? What better assistance could you seek? Follow us. If the immenseness of the mountain did not bring you relief or gratification, perhaps the diminutiveness of the butterfly will. Perhaps it was not in great deeds, or perhaps it was not in the drama of life that you found the greatest meaning. Perhaps a great enlightenment does not need to anchor itself to a great object or a great moment. Perhaps all along it was the small living things of the world which were to be your basis for wisdom and for faith. Perhaps our efforts are greater than the upheaval of the Earth that forms a mountain. Perhaps our small dips and rises in flight are more like your own soul's journey and more representative to you of what must be in your path.

My friends, I depart now. We know that there is joy within you to see us, and that faith in the unknown God is rekindled in you. We are gratified.

Be at peace with us for being most humble beings. Thank you. My friends, I depart now. We know that there is joy to see us within you, and that faith in the unknown God is rekindled in you. We are gratified.

Be at peace with us for being most humble beings. Thank you.

● The Second Descent

I t is the case that, whether you proceed forward with courage or as a coward, the sun will rise and set. As you go forward in faith and courage, the sun, nevertheless, is setting on the horizon, and your body, under the strain of the conquest and the escape from this pinnacle, is exhausted and spent. It is now that you realize the mind alone can do nothing. Yet it is not the mind now which troubles you, for faith has led the mind to a place of equanimity, while the body is still in the state of forced labor and agitation. As you climb down through the cloud layers, the mountain begins to slope down into a valley. You see little outcropping of moss and the first patches of flowers, and you are able to walk now. Although you appreciate your body's energy has been sustaining you through your journey, it is not unlimited. You need to rest, and you need nourishment.

Could it be that the call that went out to God in your climb up the mountain was so little noticed and so unworthy of response that now you will be left here at the doorway of a life unknown, unable to break through? Could it be that all your efforts have yielded not even the ability to continue in the body, so that you would not even have the time to disavow the egotism of your ascent?

The same faith needed for you to continue is now necessary for you to stop and to rest. At this time you walk. Although the slope is steep, you are able to descend it. You look above and you see the sun passing through the clouds into the horizon. There are no mountains on this far horizon. There are simply clouds formed like mountains. You are staring at the sun perhaps for the last time, because without food, without warmth, without rest, you will not be able to continue in this body, and you know it.

But then, in despair, you look for another reason to have faith. You look for a sign. You have already received one, and now you search for another. And there, not too far away, you see it.

What first appears to be a cloud rising out of the Earth, you understand to be smoke rising from a chimney. There seems to be a house nearby. It must be so. It was so cold on the mountain. You are frozen and exhausted and need some food. The body, as if some other consciousness were applied to it, starts off at a brisk gait towards the smoke. You must believe that you will find safety in that distant fire.

You work your way through the rocks and shrubs and the few trees creeping up the side of the mountain. At last you find yourself in front of a small cabin.

There is a yellow light coming from inside. Here is the source of the smoke you followed, and you knock on its door. It is I who opens it.

Relieved and exhausted, as if a gust of wind had taken the last bit of strength from out of your legs, you take one step inside the door and collapse into my arms. I take you and lay you upon a bed.

I am here. You have knocked on the door of my hermitage. You have not invaded my territory but have followed my signal and reached my outpost. If you must know, I have been like you, a mountain climber wanting to achieve great things, yet not knowing where God lies in this world. I have found some place to be, to contemplate, to reach my own inner wisdom and guidance, and to find my own soul. I have set myself here so that other souls, quite like myself, may reach some place of shelter and safety.

When I close the door, the wind blows even stronger, as if it had been reticent to harm you. It has not blown as cold and as strong as it does now. But that frigid, blustering strength is a token of your right manner in seeking refuge. I hear the wind, and I know the message that it brings. I turn to you, make you comfortable and allow you to rest. My name is not important, and in your weariness you do not attempt to ask me for it. I bring you something hot to eat that I have sitting by the fire. I throw a few clean and dry blankets on you so that you will be able to pass into the sleep which you have needed for quite some time. Unknowing, you have pushed yourself past the point of exhaustion. You fall asleep. Without sleep, your mind would have recoiled from your body.

We pass the night, and upon awakening we exchange greetings. There is more food, if you like, and you take advantage of my hospitality. This pleases me. You know instinctively that you need rest before you continue, and I instinctively offer it to you. You can take as many days or weeks as you desire to get the strength back to continue on your journey. I do not ask you to describe or explain it, because I know in my heart that you do not know the purpose of your journey or its destination.

The food tastes good. It is perhaps the best food you have taken in, although my cooking is not that wonderful. The cabin is warmer than perhaps any cabin in which you have been. The blankets are smoother than any blanket that you have ever touched. I am more than happy to engage you in conversation and just as happy to let you be, to think, and to enjoy yourself. Truly, you see that I have been comfortable in my solitude and that you cannot breach it.

Like a mug of warm wine, awareness is poured into you. You are beginning to rethink your exploration. There must be some other way to attain the unknowable. Perhaps, you believe, I will be your guidance and point you in the right direction. You make a few overtures and I repel them.

I am not your guide, my friend. I am not here to instruct you in what to do or how to do it. I am not telling you what your heart's purpose is or what you are seeking. For if you do not know what you are seeking, I cannot help you. I am here to provide those comforts to your body which will enable you to go forward. So you turn away from me in silence. I have rebuffed you, and you seek some other help. You see that along the wall of my cabin I have many books. It is a crude cabin, but I am not a crude man. "Stand up and see," I suggest to you, "the many written works that have inspired and aided me." You take me up on my offer and scan the bookshelves, seeking some clue as to who you are and what you are to do. One by one you take out my books and explore them. Reading becomes very pleasant for you. If you cannot find the answers, maybe you can find someone else who has found them or at least you may realize that you are not the only fool in the world. You see how others have tried and failed. You read voraciously, and you are much nourished. You are as nourished by the written word as you are by the humble food I serve.

Weeks pass. I have been serious about making you welcome, but you know that you will not stay forever. At one point, as you come in from helping me with my chores and begin to browse through the bookshelf again, you pick out a certain book and open it up. On its inside cover there is the stamp of a bookstore, and suddenly you are aware of something which had not occurred to you. You realize that my life is not the life of one entirely isolated, and that I have come from somewhere, and that I go back occasionally to that place from where I have come. There may be, indeed, another town beyond my tiny cabin.

Surely I do not grow all of my food and make all of my clothes. "Why have you not thought of this before?" I reply, as you ask me from where the book has come. You say simply that perhaps you did not even think that there was anything beyond the small town from which you have come. Your curiosity now is so piqued that you ask if I would be willing to take you there the next time I go to get some provisions. I agree that tomorrow will be a fine day for this. You settle down and wait for the dawn, enthralled in the thought that perhaps the mystery will be solved if you follow the trail of the book to its point of origin. Perhaps the place is a rightful one for the mind to grow, for you to ask and receive answers to nagging questions about who you are and what God is or where God is. Now you know that these questions must be addressed.

Rest well, my friend, for tomorrow I take you to your destination. Good night.

The Second Descent

● The Third Descent

With your rescuer at your side, you round the crest of the last hill, and before you lies the village. It seems to be quite an inviting place, nestled between the mountain from which you have come and the deep broad lake on its opposite side. You pick up your steps and together you walk down the hill to the entrance road to town. You have carried with you an empty sack, hoping to fill it with written knowledge from this place. The roads leading from the surrounding countryside to the town are filled with small farms and shops and a few houses scattered here and there. And, as you get closer, the landscape becomes more complex. The number of people visible increases, until you recognize that you are in the town proper amongst houses and buildings which seem quite well established and ordered. The architecture and the layout of the city are all rather familiar to you. The roofs are the roofs of the place which you have left, peaked and narrow. You see that the widths of the streets are varied according to the density of the traffic, and this is also something familiar.

As you move into the heart of the city, you feel the onset of a realization, the nature of which you are not quite sure. Here at its hub, a circular road in which is set a small park, you find the chamber of commerce building. It is a natural place to begin, a place where you believe you may find the resources for you to continue onward, resources which have been the subject of your thoughts for so long.

You walk into the lobby of the building seeking help. By chance, you find me. And when you do, instinctively you know that it is time for you to part from your host. He has done enough already. And you know that you can take yourself on this leg of your journey without guidance. You bid him adieu.

You do, however, have an awkward situation at hand. I appear to you to be quite learned and officious; you on the other hand, feel yourself to be unknowing, powerless and without direction. You have to explain where you have come from and what you have been doing without frankly stating the purpose of your journey, or even the nature of your experience, because you have yet to come to this understanding. I am the mayor of this small town, and a fairly jolly fellow I am. I bid you welcome, and when I do, it is with a certain amount of aplomb and affability, but I am not the fool that you are. I am not so foolish to think, for instance, that I hold the answers for you. I know in some ways that it is impossible to find your answers outside yourself. But I hold this to myself, and we engage in a conversation. You describe your journey: you were searching for something and could not discover it. That is sufficient for me. And now you find yourself here after being close to death and being found by your kind companion, with whom I, too, am acquainted. You realize the limitations of my relationship with you. I cannot be your other guide, but what I can do is to demonstrate to you, again, that there are things ahead of you which you cannot possibly imagine, maybe wonderful things. Maybe my cheerfulness is a sign to you that there could be many happy experiences yet for you.

I will show you all the things to do and to see in my city. In a deeper sense, I am showing you all the things that others have experienced and the manifestations drawn from those experiences—the cathedral, the central plaza, the botanical gardens, the zoo, the stores with their silks and linens, the markets with their fruits and smoked meats, the manner of dress that we have, our way of speaking, what we imagine ourselves to be doing here, our mottos and colloquialisms, our heroes and our villains. I can put these in your hand one after another, there being a pamphlet for each. And, at first you think that these manifestations are extraordinarily tedious and petty things about which to be conversant. You, the great explorer, do not care or could not have patience for this. It is belittling to you. But then you begin to understand that my purpose is to bring homage to those who have toiled and those who have achieved in this place. And each small pamphlet that I put in your hand is a reminder that others have

The Third Descent

arrived somewhere, where you do not seem to be so able to settle down.

At some point, I believe that I have spoken enough and that you need time to digest what I have said. I take you by the shoulder, move you out the door, and show you the view of the plaza from the chamber. Here you can choose what life you would like to lead. Any kind of life that you would choose is represented in this town—the church, the vegetable market, the little restaurant where they serve tea in small cups and little bits of something to eat, the parks, the playgrounds, the schools, and the fire house. What a world it is. But, what is the prosaic world? You do not really know, because you do not know anything else but the prosaic world, I remind you. You have not much of anything against which to compare it.

So, perhaps you are meant to stay in such a place and to relax. It is an interesting proposition. You think, "Perhaps I should never have left my home. Or, perhaps, instead I have found a better place, a truer place, where I can flourish." Cheered, you shake my hand and we depart.

I know what you will do. You will be the tourist and set out on a trek with your little map. Indeed, you walk and walk through the streets without real direction, taking in with your eyes all the town's activities.

The sun shines carelessly. The day is warm. You really do not have a care in the world either. You take a break from your walking and sit down on a bench to have something to eat. A fruit vendor comes along and you buy some nourishing fruit with some cream on it. A child has thrown a ball against your feet; you pick it up and throw it back. This is the spot for you. This place is making your old desires and you yourself seem quite foolish again. You can, you think, go back to this life. All the traveling, all the exertion, the hardships, the pain, the nagging unknowing, and the fear, what purpose did they have? Why could you not settle down here, or in a place like this? What is life about, but the simple things?

Again, you get up, and you begin to walk around. But, a certain feeling begins to overtake you. It is, oddly, one of remorse. You think, "Is it sadness because I have lost something? I had a home like this. I had a place on which I turned my back. I could have been starting to have a family or a meaningful job. I did not need to make this journey." Then, in the realization of this thought, you find yourself in deeper sadness. And you begin, not to question your heart, but to question what it is you are seeing.

There on the corner is a teenager. He reminds you of someone whom you once knew in school. He stands on the street corner as if anticipating recognition of his cunning and virility, but it does not come. You seem to know this person. You look to the side. There is a storekeeper sweeping out some debris from the sidewalk onto the street. He is working intensely and with haste. He seems to be the kind of person who is perpetually anxious, and perhaps he is. Is this man not just like the man who ran the library where you lived? In fact, as your eyes begin to open, you see that the place in which you are is the place from which you have come, except everything is juxtaposed. The library here was the municipal building at home. The church was the temple. The police officer was the school teacher.

This town is really no different from what you have known all of your life. It is as if everyone has misplaced his or her identity and has taken up a new one at random. In fact, this point is brought home to you even more forcefully by the manner in which people greet you. They greet you as if they have known you all of their lives. It is more than friendliness; it is familiarity with which you do not know what to do. You return the greeting and smile but something more begins to trouble you. You realize that the sadness coming out from you is quite deep. You realize that in most significant ways you have returned to your point of origin. The town has a different name as well as the people, but it is the same place. The cars look a bit funny, but they have the same colors and contours. The customs are different, the manners are different, but they are the same customs and manners. In fact, you look back now and you see the mountain in the distance and you see a shadow cast now not on the town square, but on the circular park in the town plaza. And you know that no one pays attention to the mountain here anymore than they did back home.

This is a time of great grieving for you. You believe that your journey has been fruitless. You have been a dog chasing its tail, and now you have caught it. Here you are in the town of mirror images and mirror games—a house of mirrors. You half expect to see a different you emerging from a doorway, greeting you on the street with a solemn "Hello."

It is grieving that you experience in this deep state. It is grieving for the fool who went to the mountain without knowing why, without understanding self, and returning as ignorant as before. It is the fool who does not know what he has learned and what he has not learned. It is the fool who does not know the nature of God at work. Everything that you see seems to be drained of meaning. There is a hollowness in the smiling faces and the gestures. The emptiness of the mountain seems to have been poured out into the streets, filling the people with a dreaded meaninglessness. What have you been doing and why?

You are not going to find the answers here now as a visitor. You decide that certain steps must be taken. Surely you can retrieve some inner meaning from what you have done, where you have gone, and why you have been there. But, how are you to get this?

Your feet now seem to work for you in a way they have not before. They seem to be able to unscramble the city's layout and to find their way through it to your destination. As they propel you forward, you suddenly recall that your intent in coming here was a search for knowledge, which you believed was most necessary. It was the book with the imprint upon it that led you to think that your answers were in this small town.

Your feet now slow you down and bring you to a stop. You have turned a corner, and you see that before you and above you is a sign. It is the book vendor's sign. And to your left you see an expanse of window behind which are books of every size and description: books of plants and paintings, books of health and history, books of romance and rebellions. You decide it is here in which everything you have known in this town and in your home has coalesced. The sum of all knowledge that one can have as the result of abiding in any such place as this is behind that glass.

You decide to investigate. Your answer must lie there. If it does not, then surely you are a lost soul.

My friend, I leave you now to your next encounter and hope and trust that I have been of service. Thank you.

● The Fourth Descent

W e bring you greetings. I am here in the rear of the store into which you are about to walk. You do not see me yet, but I am here. I wait for you, although you do not know that any-one is waiting for you. But I most certainly am, even if my waiting is not just for you. You enter with the appearance of a hungry god thirst-ing for knowledge, and you scan the bookshelves.

You are here because all that must be is represented in some form in these books before you. What you quest is what we also per-ceive to be here. Indeed, the answer to the question, "What is your quest?" is here for you. You feel it and you know it. Soon, we will verify it, but it will not be in the way you anticipate.

You have been on a fool's journey. And, what has been kept from you on this fool's journey? Well, you have made mistakes, I imag-ine. You have pursued vapors and dreams and chased after clouds. But one thing that the fool most needs is to be laughed at. And here I am. I am here to laugh at you.

What a greeting! From the well of all knowledge, from the sciences, from philosophy and metaphysics, from the rigors of math-ematics, from all the depths of human experience and knowledge, I am here to laugh at you. You, the young god, placing one foot tenu-ously in front of another, placing a hand on one book after another, as if they are handholds on a mountain climb, make your way towards the back of the building. Touching each book in anticipation of what will be uncovered from the wisdom of the ages, you decide you need a map, a philosophical stance. You need something yet undefined. You need some point of view that you have not yet had.

You work your way as if through a stand of trees, as though the paper in the books had not yet been made into paper but is still wood, and the store is yet a forest. You make your way through the aisles toward the back, thinking that there is a clearing in the back and that you will be able to concentrate and open your mind. Instead, you see a counter, a register and a rather becoming woman behind the register. She smiles in the same way everyone has been smiling to you in the town, as if her face had been stamped by the same hand. She is not me, but you meet me soon.

Here in this place are some selected books thought to be of the greatest interest to the greatest number of people. It is as good a starting point as is possible, and you begin to browse through them. Suddenly, something hits your head. You look down. It is a piece of food— a banana. You shake yourself. "It must have been lying on the floor all this time. Some child must have dropped it." And you continue your browsing. Then, something hits your face and tumbles down your chest onto the floor. You look down—it is a nut. You look up before you and see nothing. You again take up your browsing. Then, all of sudden, something hits your back quite hard. You turn around. A small book, but a book nevertheless, has been thrown at your back. You search about. What could this be? There are few people in the store, and they seem to be even more proper and composed than you are. You look and you do not see any wobbly shelves; the store does not seem to have any part falling down on you. And then, you hear me. "Ha, ha, ha!" We are laughing. "Ha, ha, ha!" It is a sharp laugh but a sincere one, an animated laughter which is laughter more intense than any you have heard to date in this valley. "Ha, ha, ha!" It is the most sincere and heartfelt expression that you have ever heard. It is my laughter, and I laugh with you, but I must confess, my friend, that I am laughing at you.

You made such an easy target of yourself for my bananas and nuts that I thought a whole book would be the best thing to throw at you next. For you truly are a fool to stand there and to receive it.

You look up. Finally, you recognize your attacker; you catch sight of me. I am sitting on the very top of the bookshelves behind you. And when you see me, I laugh again, I jump up and down and I run back to the counter. You go to the register and to the comely lady behind it and say, "You have a monkey in your bookstore." "Yes, indeed, we do. I hope he has not caused you trouble," she says properly. "No," you say, lying. I laugh when you say no. I am sitting on her shoulder and looking at you and making faces. I try to approximate your bewildered look. "Ha, ha, ha!" "It seems rather strange," you say, "to have a monkey in a bookstore." "Oh," she says, "he is a little nuisance, but he will not bother you much. He rarely bothers the customers." As if to prove her wrong, I jump up and down and scurry onto the counter and jump onto your chest and work my way around your shoulders and stand on your head. Then I jump onto a ceiling fan which is slowly spinning above you. And, turning around and around as if it is a merry-go-round, I use it to leap to another section of books where I sit as if I am the Buddha in meditation. "I cannot imagine anything stranger," you think to yourself, "than a monkey in a bookstore."

Here, in this reservoir of knowledge which literature provides, there is this idiotic animal, mocking and teasing. "What can its purpose be?" You only think this, but your thoughts are loud, and I respond. Another piece of banana gets thrown on your head, and I hurry around the corner so you will not catch me. The monkey must be saying something to you. "Oh, no, is it possible," you ask, "that the monkey is my next sign? I have been following signs all the time and now I am reduced to the monkey sign. The monkey is to give me what message-the message that I have little worth, that I am this fool, that I am to be laughed at?" You are taking this monkey very seriously.

You round the corner. Maybe if you pick up Aristotle, the monkey will not throw anything at you, or so you hope. Aristotle is there on shelf B. You pick up Aristotle. I throw a rolled-up bit of paper at you. You put down Aristotle. "Monkeys come from the Orient," you say. "Let us work our way over to Eastern philosophy. I will pick up a copy of the Sutras. Now, what is your response?" I jump on your head and I run off. "Well," you say, "the Sutras do me no good." Then, as if saying an oath, you place your hand upon a stack of Bibles. You look around. I am nowhere to be seen. "This must be the answer," you say. Then, down at your feet, you feel a tugging. I am there. "Ha, ha, ha!" I laugh again and scurry around your feet and run off.

You are amazed. Every deep question which you have put to me I have answered. I have answered with such incredible directness and sophistication, it has amazed you. I go make for myself another perch on shelf G, and you start to contemplate me. I, of course, am contemplating you and hoping that you will still remain the fool at whom I can throw something. But I will wait and not spend all my laughter in one fool's minute. "Ha, ha, ha!"

You begin to think, "There is kind of a transcendent air to this animal. He is comfortable in the bookstore and yet he is not obligating himself to all that knowledge. He has a playful answer to all the questions that the books raise. He has a response that is an inner response. And, he has assuredness in this. He knows what he is; he knows what he is not. He is not a scholar. He seems to be a scholar's foil. But, yet, he seems to be possessed of some wisdom." And, you begin to wonder where I have gotten it, do you not?

I have been around many places. I have gone on many journeys myself. I am not afraid to be the fool—you are. I am not afraid to be above that which seems to be above the ordinary. I am the monkey, and I know it. I have grace and beauty, in my own way, and laughter in ways that you cannot predict. I am still sitting here. Maybe I am not the sitting Buddha. Maybe I am the Thinker. "Ha, ha, ha!" My head rests on my hand, with an elbow propped on my knee. "Ha, ha, ha!" Oh, how I mock you. Or, maybe I mock everyone and you are the only one who notices. Have I piqued your curiosity? What have I experienced that has made me like this? Perhaps you need to get rid of all your baggage right now, your mental baggage in any case, and I am a way for you to do it. You do not know—perhaps I have come from a place which has provided me with a great many lessons, and these cannot be reproduced in the world which you have witnessed so far. Perhaps I come from a place in which we do not pause to learn but find learning to be part of breathing in life, where we take in wisdom as we breathe. Perhaps not. Perhaps I am just a better fool than you are, showing you your humble position even while being a fool myself.

"Ha, ha, ha!" I laugh now because I can read this thought occurring to you as I think it myself. You walk over to the counter again. "From where does your monkey come?" you ask. The comely lady is astounded that you would ask such a question. "Why, the monkey comes from the jungle, of course. This and all monkeys come from the jungle." "Where is the jungle?" you ask. "Is it close by?" Once again, she looks at you as if you are the most ignorant man she has ever met. "Why, of course," she says, "the jungle is on the other side of the lake. But no one goes there. It is too dangerous a place. If you take a journey by boat on the lake, you will surely reach it, but I would advise against it," she says. "Do you have a map?" you ask. Now, a few paces behind you, I am jumping up and down, laughing. "Of course not!" she exclaims. "Who would want to go into the jungle? There are so many things for us to do here. We do not need to go on such a perilous journey, full of tigers and who knows what." "Can you show me the lake?" you ask. And she says, "Of course. Now the lake is something beautiful, although who knows what is really on its far distant shores?" This lake has been mapped and she shows it to you. "You are here," she says, "and here is the dock on the lake from which all people depart."

Now you are excited. I hear you, and I begin to think of you as a countryman. You and I, perhaps someday, could sit on top of the books together and throw them down at people when they pass by. Perhaps you will learn what I have learned in the place from which I have come. Perhaps you will enjoy my talk a little bit more, knowing that you are at the end of your fool's journey because you have reached the pinnacle of foolishness. In speaking to me now, you show your wish to have me with you. Perhaps we could have a little drink together. Perhaps we shall dine out. "Do you like bananas?" I ask in my mind and I laugh out loud. But I know in my heart that you must go away. You turn and you walk out the door. Before you go, however, you say good-bye to me. I do a somersault for you. This is our way of saying good-bye. And I wish you well, my friend; you are on a journey that is an exquisite wonder. I should know—I have been there before.

I will stay and wait for the next soul who can come and listen. We have been exchanging a great many ideas, and you need to act upon those thoughts to which I have guided you. My soul is with you.

Good-bye.

The Fifth Descent

S o, it is at the urging of the monkey that you leave the bookstore. And, in fact, you bid farewell to the town, as you work your way down through the alleys, by warehouses, and past railway crossings to the lake front, the wharves, and the quays. Truly, it is a pretty lake. You cannot imagine a place of greater peace or calm. The lake, placid and still, offers no resistance to your eyes. You cannot see through its waters, but you are not disturbed by its opacity. You stand on a small dock looking into the horizon. The lake stretches out so far that you cannot see the distant shore. You sense the jungle calling to you from that faraway place.

There is peace and calm here which you have not experienced in quite some time. It is a paradox that you are making what is to be the last leg of your journey in great anticipation, and yet the expectation of further adventure does not cause nervousness or anxiety. In fact, something in the nature of the lake calls you to be as placid as it is. You sit with your legs dangling off the dock. The sack that you brought with you to fill with the world's great books is empty, but your heart is not disconsolate. It is full of promise and warmth. In the far distance the sun is beginning to set and, although you cannot imagine now where you will be sleeping, the expectation of peaceful slumber is most welcomed.

But you wait and wait even more. Behind you and to the same extent it is far from you, there is activity. Work is being finished up for the evening. People are running home to their quarters, running home to eat and to sleep. The lake water is cool but not frigid, cool and unresisting to your feet as you wave your toes in it.

As the sun continues to set and your eyes continue to be fixed on the western horizon, you begin to distinguish a small figure in the distance.

It is someone standing in a boat. As it draws nearer, the outlines of the figure become more readily discernible. The boat, in approaching, brings a pleasant but surprising calm. In some place in your mind you have known of this encounter, although at this point you have no inkling of its nature. The boat draws closer and closer. As it does, the sun's rays become dimmer. The sky, which is clear, except for a few long clouds at the horizon, is becoming orange, red, and then purple as time transpires. As the light from the horizon meets the blue sky, the fire of the sun turns it smoky and gray.

The boat approaches as if it has always known it is to come to you, and you have known its purpose is to bear you away, to take you from the dock and the town, take you from your memories, take you from the emptiness of the mountain. But no one speaks to you from the boat and no one will. At some point you wonder whether death is coming for you. For there is such a stillness in the figure on the small boat and such a blackness that it is barely to be distinguished from the lake. But, as you breathe into this thought, it dissipates. It is not death coming for you. This is a different sleep. You wait patiently and happily.

At last, the boat draws very close to the dock, and you see that the boatman is tall and lean. He has a long pole which he has just picked up from the bottom of the boat, and with it he is now directing the boat to the dock. It is I who is coming for you, and it is I who have been waiting for you out in the middle of the lake. I am the boatman, and if you were to take the time to look around you at all the people of this town which you visited, you will see that there is not one of them who could recognize me, for I have been waiting for you alone. You grasp this. You see me quite singularly in your own mind. You cannot mistake me for anyone else but someone whose mission is to be with you this evening. You cannot do so, because there is no one else who could perceive me. You speculate that I must be yours. And, you are correct. I am to bear you away from this place.

In what reality do we exist? Is there more than one? You are not sure. But you are world-weary. You are tired of your conceits and your ambitions. You look toward us for salvation. We are dressed in simple clothes—dark pants and cloak are all that is visible. My gaunt features are friendly but removed. The prow of the boat bumps up against a pier that supports the dock. I lean against my pole, and with the other hand, I stretch out a palm to you. Without words, I am inviting you to make this voyage with me. I am your relief. You have always known that there was some means in and some means out of any situation where you feel entrapped. But you have never seen anything quite like this.

You cast a glance behind you. There are a few people left on the shoreline, doing their manual labor or whatever it will take to settle their affairs for the day. But they do not see you and they do not see me. You turn and put one foot in, then the other, and you sit. I smile and turn the boat around. We are going. The sun, ever closer to the horizon, is a brilliant red now, and it is like a sign for this mysterious place to which you will be going. But the sensation of the buoyant force of the waters and the aura of the lake are overwhelming your anticipation of the jungle. You must simply be in this boat, gently rocked by it, and in its power at the moment.

There is a feeling of peace and calm with you which you could not have known before. There is nothing in the least unsteady about the boat as it slips past the waterfront and into the dark womb of the waters. And, now, you begin to drift into contemplation, as your eyes begin to feel heavy. The lake itself has been calling to you all this time. Like the mountain before it, the lake has infected your impulses. It has driven you toward it without you being cognizant of it. It has pulled you to its heart without your knowing why or how. The lake in blackness now shows its shape to you. It is neither a blackness of evil nor one of concealment; it is one of deep revelation.

The water has risen up to be a lake, into the shape of the mountain reversed. The lake is an inversion of the mountain. As much as the mountain stretched up in emptiness to the heavens, the lake stretches down in fulfillment to the Earth. The lake is speaking directly to your mind, your heart, and your soul. It is, after all, so vast that it has much to say, and it gives itself much time in which to say it. It is prolific.

I, your boatman, with my back to you, continue to push the boat with my pole. But soon I let go the pole, securing it to the rear, and picking up a long oar, I begin to paddle. I maintain my silence, for at this point, there is nothing enlightening for me to say to you. And you are drifting off anyway. The lake has better, more profound words to say. The deepness of things does not always signify profundity, but in this lake there is great profundity. You have no resentment for the words which are spoken by the water that laps at the side of the boat. They are insistent yet gentle. Your eyes become heavier, and you see behind you that the shorelines of the lake are completely gone from your vision. They have slipped over the horizon, and you must be in the center of this lake. It seems as if you are adrift. The night sky above you has few stars. There are few reflections in the water. It is not busy.

As your eyes become heavy, you think back to the place you were born, or imagine you were born. Was it not that you suddenly remembered yourself to be alive? You opened your eyes and found yourself somewhere, and then as soon as you did, you departed. Was it not that the journey to the mountain, as arduous as it was, was quite dreamlike and intangible? The cutting, cold pain in your lungs when you reached the peak, the wind that you felt in your hair, around your head, and up your back—was it not like a bitter mirage? The journey down from the mountain and the finding of everything that you seemed to have wanted—except that you did not know yourself and could not truly find what you wanted—was it not like a meditation of soul? And you think, now, that perhaps your insistence all this time that you knew you were alive and you knew the world was real, was somehow flawed. Your remembrance is telling you that perhaps you have only been dreaming yourself, and you have been afloat on a dream, a dream like this lake that has shape but has no shape, that is deep as the mountain is high but is formless water.

Can you dream? Are you dreaming now? What could you be? Could you be soul? Could you be God? If you are not God, where is God? The heavens are unyielding to your vision; you do not see anything there. And the boat affords you no real vista of the lake. You are in this middle place between realms, but between which realms you do not know. If God is above, you do not feel below. If God is with you, then what have you been remembering—the dream of God? If there is no God, there must only be emptiness. And in this emptiness there must be great pain. But you are not sitting on emptiness—you are between. You are between whatever you would call heaven and whatever you would call Earth, floating and happy for it. No, this is not another form of emptiness. Perhaps you have found the antidote to emptiness, but it could not itself be empty.

I look back at you and remind you of your own thoughts. If the mountain has brought you emptiness, its watery mirror image has brought you fullness, but it is as weighty and impenetrable as the rock of the mountain. This fullness, now, is yielding water. It is shapeless and your hand can pass through it. What a strange thought that the only thing which can be real is that which is the most dreamlike. What you have believed to be fixed, permanent, and dense has been vapor, and what could be so amorphous and illusive comes to you as being whole and alive.

The lake is alive, but it is alive in your dream. You know that you have been wrong, and in your pursuit of what is behind the apparent, you have fallen into a dream, the dream of your own making. You imagined that, because you thought, you existed. But you know now that you exist because you dream. You dream because you are a soul dreaming self and nothing else. You have dreamed your adventure. You have dreamed your pain. You have dreamed your complacency, and you have dreamed your unhappiness. And yet your eyes become even heavier. "If this is the dream, I must understand who is dreaming." The jungle, you suppose, is no more real than what you have experienced. Maybe it is less so, because you need to pass through this lake of dreams to get to it. The jungle is in your mind now, but in your mind it will stay. It is the product of your dreaming. It is the culmination of dreaming. It is your journey's end and your journey's beginning, both at the same time.

You lapse into sleep. Can you dream inside the dream? You try. You fail. But your body needs refreshment and nourishment, and you sleep.

Upon awakening, you see the shoreline of the jungle. The few rays of dawn silhouette the outlines of the trees and cast a few birds to flight in your direction. You are refreshed in a way that you could not have imagined yourself to be. The boat is going toward the shore. You feel almost as if you can stand up, and you do. As I take my pole once again and direct the boat through shallow waters, you jump off and wade waist-deep through the waves to the shore. You turn, and we say good-bye with a few gestures.

I have been your guide. I have led you on this voyage. I am of the angelic realm, the Archangel Lemmiel, who leads you to sleep and to wake at the same time. Whenever you call, my presence will be with you. I leave you now as you turn toward the shore.

My friends, you need not have any trepidation about meeting my kind. We are here to guide you to that inner place which you could not find by yourself. We leave you to your own devices in it. You cannot know the beauty and the wonder that will await you. You do not understand that all the journeys you take bring you nowhere. Until you find that inner journey, all journeys will be meaningless. We leave you at this point.

Good-bye. May you go with God.

PART FOUR
The Jungle

Preface

You are blessed with many jungles on this planet. You do not know this, but it is a rarity in the universe to have so many exotic, beautiful jungles and rain forests dense with vegetation and animal life. So, we would like to begin your journey in this context. The journey of the mind is like a journey through the jungle. As you grow in this life, your mind begins to become like a jungle, does it not? We say that every thought which is planted inside your mind is like a seed which has taken root and sprouted forth in a jungle. Some bear great fruit, others have great beauty. Some are like vines twisting around trees or other forms of vegetation. Some are not evident in their purpose. Some offer shade, and you wish only to sit under them. There are, likewise, animals in the jungle. Creatures feed upon those seeds of thought that have been planted inside your mind. Animals cavort with each other, or perhaps prey on each other.

The things of the jungle are things of your mind. Have you never listened to a wonderful lecture in school and, having listened to it, felt as though there was a thought planted, like a seed, inside you? And you have relished the idea that this seed will take root and sprout forth a beautiful flowering plant. Perhaps this has worked out, and perhaps it has not. Perhaps it was an interesting diversion. You also know that you have planted your own seeds in this jungle of your mind. In this way, you know that you are responsible for those thoughts and feelings which you have locked up inside.

You know that in this stage of your life you are not young children anymore. The forest has become very dense and complex. There is great symbiosis between those elements which have been planted inside this jungle. A nineteenth century mind would say that a jungle is wilderness, beyond the rational world; that the jungle exists in chaos, in wildness. But you are not in this stage now. You see things in terms of symbiotic relationships. You see one element of the environment as relating to all others. In the same way, you are now looking at the mind. You are not lost—and we are not trying to induce you to be lost in some wilderness. Rather, we want you to explore, to appreciate the complexity and the interdependence of all those elements inside you.

You may stop now and say to me, "I have read so far, and I am not comfortable with the idea that I have planted something and it is there to stay. Suppose I wish to get rid of something in this jungle of my mind. Suppose something no longer serves me, like a thought that I have outgrown. Perhaps it is a thought of greed, egotism, anger or hatred, or power and dominance over others." We can tell you that you are more than privileged to take a machete and hack away at the foliage in your path, the foliage which you no longer wish to be there, or which seems to be hurting something else in this garden world. This is your privilege. It is your jungle after all. However, we say this to you: despite the fact that you wish to eliminate these things from your mind, ask yourself if you truly wish to eliminate the experience of having had those things in your jungle. In other words, if you have been greedy in your life and have valued money above all things, you may now wish to change. So, you go through a process of healing. Now you will no longer have this greed tree which is dark and corrupted in your jungle. It is cut down, you see. But there is a stump left, is there not? And from the stump there may sprout a tree of great, generous limbs. In other words, while you want to get rid of those artifacts of the mind that no longer serve you, nevertheless, do you truly wish to deny the experience of having had those things inside you? You would, likewise, eliminate the growth that has happened through them. You would eliminate greater understanding.

Your position now is not to judge what is in your jungle, and it is not for us to send you a message of how terrible your jungle is. How many difficulties do you have in there? How many misconceptions? We do not care. We are not here to have you judge your jungle;

we are here to help you work through it. And you work through it only as you travel through it. The jungle will take care of itself.

At the end of your journey, you will find yourself in a new realm. This realm is one of experience only. It will not make sense as a story. One day you may be at the water's edge; another, you are flying in the sky; another, you are at the depths of the sea; another, you are an angel; another, you are a peasant woman; another you are God. You must see yourself everywhere. But, take yourself through this forest first.

We wish you love and blessings.

The Bird of Paradise

The First Node

We greet you in love and joy. I am a devic being and my purpose and intent in coming to you and speaking will make itself manifest as time goes on in our little story. All devic beings attach themselves to one or a number of entities upon the planet and serve them. We do not or will not interfere with the free will of the souls whom we serve. And it is our intent to speak to you, to let you know that our purpose is not to control or to influence you either, but to guide and illuminate.

It will soon become apparent to which entities I belong. However, I want first to start you on your journey in the jungle. I am representing to you the first node. I am the entity who, of all entities, can best represent this.

I wish to take you to the beginning of your journey. You have disembarked and are standing on the edge of an incredibly vast, intricate forest. You do not feel afraid. You can sense the myriad life forms before you. Beauty which has been unimaginable is now in front of you. You did not know what you might expect when you began this journey. And, now, here on the verge of entering the jungle, you are already feeling a great reward just for the idea that you are willing to begin. There are sounds. There are visions. Yet, you cannot penetrate the complexity of this jungle with the eyes and ears alone, or certainly not from the vantage point at which you find yourself. You must go within this forest. There is light, and there is heat. The heat of the jungle is that of your emotions. The light which illuminates is that force which powers your whole being. You take in when you breathe. It replenishes and nourishes. This is a beautiful time. Anxious to begin, you pick up your steps and enter the jungle.

This jungle is your mind. You know this at the first step, and you know it at the last step. But, nevertheless, you are seeing it for the first time, perhaps, as something that you may have created, something that you can appreciate in and of itself. You are a wanderer through your own mind, needing to know and to understand it. The first node is one of creating a new self. You are creating a sensation of objectivity. You are taking apart that which was so readily built up in mind. You are beginning to discern it. Your journey is something of a scientific one.

We say to you, as you go through the jungle, you will find many intricate paths. You do not want to trip and fall on any rock or root protruding from the ground. You need sometimes to use a broad knife to cut the plants in your path. Nevertheless, this downward gaze which you sometimes have, this practical attitude, does not mitigate your sense of purpose. Your goal, your vision is, in fact, a lofty one. So much so, that as you go on this journey, you begin to look up right away. Your gaze is heavenward. And, what are amongst the high branches of those trees around you? What is calling to you? What seems to stand out with great brilliance, with beautiful, sharp, true colors—the truest colors in the world? They are those beings you call birds.

In the jungle, bird life is most elegant, most colorful, most exciting. Of those beings in the jungle you call birds, the ones to whom I have attached myself are the most beautiful of all. We are the deva of the bird of paradise. The first thing you notice as you go through this jungle is the bird of paradise. What are we? We are to you that which is the highest, that which is the most beautiful, whose light seems to shine on in greatest abundance, with greater force than anything else. In this jungle we are the vision of God, the sound of God, the experience of the God Light in your own soul, that which is in you and in every aspect of your self.

In your mind, as in the jungle, the vision and the thought of God is most apparent, like a bird of paradise. We hold your attention so much that perhaps you will stumble now on protruding roots. We call out to you in a language which you do not understand. This language does not seem to have melody or cadence. It is one of mystery, for the face of God is inscrutable. You cannot know God in your life, can you? You cannot even know that part of God which is an aspect of mind. But this does not stop you from experiencing in joy the Light of God coming to you. It will not stop you from going forward, although, we say to you, is there a need to go forward from this point?

You always are judging yourselves in this manner. You always discipline your mind. You go to churches, do you not? You kneel down in prayer and you try to focus your mind on God above all things. And then you go through your week of work and play, hoping that this understanding, this connection with God will sustain you throughout the week. We say you misjudge yourselves, for you have an experience or a vision of God which is yet inside you. This is the first thing that you truly experience.

In the mind, your intent is always to the highest thing. Everyone wants to do work in their life that has a lofty purpose. Everyone intends good in this world. Even though your vision in the jungle is a lofty one—at least in the beginning— you yet may stumble upon lowly things. All beings have some lofty vision for themselves, an inherent understanding of God's presence, even if they fall. They may not choose to use the word God. They may use "morality". They may use "the universe". They may use funny phrases to describe God; nevertheless, the vision is there. It cannot be taken away. Who can pass through the jungle and not see this brightly plumed bird—not hear it, not appreciate it? It is not possible.

So, everyone intends to do wonderfully beautiful things. But they fall, and they stumble on roots in the path. They hit up against the rocks protruding from the soil. They run into obstacles which they do not always know how to handle. You question yourself, at this point, about experiencing such great beauty and knowledge just from this one event. "Do I need to proceed forward?" And our response to you is, you never do. You never do, but you will.

And so, armed with this vision of God, of paradise, you begin to open your eyes then, to the rest of the jungle. For what is it? Leaf by leaf, stem by stem, bug by bug, and creature by creature—it is that which you hold in the mind. It is you, and yet you see it as not you. You cannot walk through it by owning everything in it. You must go through it by disavowing any attachment to all that you see. This only makes sense. You cannot go through this jungle like those who must cherish greedily every little experience as if they are counting their golden hoard. Rather, you go like a breeze through everything.

You see things, as we say, somewhat scientifically. The heat of the sun is providing a sensation that is new, however. And, this heat beats down and around you. Its thick humidity is something to which you are not accustomed. Your attempt, perhaps, to be the botanist or the biologist of this jungle, to be a most objective person, is being pressured by the ambient heat which you are now feeling. Sweat, you see, is forming on your brow. And, you do not know at this point whether it is most important to take notes about what you see, or most important to experience what you are encountering in its pristine beauty and wonder.

Do we follow you? We most certainly do. We are everywhere in the branches high above you. We call. And, if we do not turn our heads to see you, we still call to you. It is the voice of God speaking to you about paradise. Where is this paradise, my friends? It is not a lost paradise. No one can speak of paradise without having contained in that communication, paradise itself. Perhaps we have come from this place, but now we bring this place to you. So that you know this, be frank with yourself. There is a part of paradise in you. You have come from this place. There is the taste of it on your tongue. There is a sensation of it in your ears. You can discern it with your eyes. You bring this with you in your mind, because you are of paradise. You move back toward it, perhaps. But you are of it. And you bring part of it with you.

So, my friends, I wish to state that we are so happy to have been able to say our piece to you. We ask you to remember that everything which follows is a result of your willingness to move toward the Divine which is already part of your experience of life. Your willingness to go into the mind has been a willingness to explore the Divine. Remember, you will not be troubled by what is the complexity of the jungle. First comes this wonderful vision. You are not troubled in this part of the journey or weighed down by the pain and drudgery of a long trek through a wilderness. You are rather refreshed and excited by this vision of heavenly beauty. I am so happy to be this entity for you, and so happy to impart to you this essence. We are together, even though I fly. Together we travel throughout the face of this Earth. Those souls who do not speak to you in words that you comprehend, journey with you. We travel with you as your companions. We are your friends. And, we present to you now another friend.

The second node is at once beautiful and terrible. Go with God.

◓ The Second Node

I speak to you from the heart of the forest. This jungle that you have embraced in your travels is a great one. Although I am in this heart, it is not a dark heart, as you know, nor an evil one. Your fear is not of the jungle itself now, but perhaps it is of me. Let me explain.

As you are continuing in your travels, you notice those things around you in the form of plants and animals. There is great complexity to all these things. And, yet, these are only things which you have created. You begin to understand their creation and how they are working together. You begin to comprehend. There seems to be order in this jungle. In fact, this jungle's order is one that you seem to be creating all of the time. You are creating it, and you have always been creating it. There is a desire for order in all beings. All beings create in order to fulfill a purpose, in order to achieve certain ends. You have studied scripture, perhaps; you have studied science. In your mind these studies are like the foliage—complex, interrelated. You begin to establish certain orders among them.

There is a point, you see, in which ideas, suggestions, intuitive thoughts, and dreams start to take hold. Seeds are planted and sprout forth vines, flowers, and trees. These which have taken hold start to have essence, or meaning in themselves. They are artifacts of the mind.

They now seem to be more powerful than you are. Who would challenge the strength of a tree? You would only knock your head against it. It would be a foolish effort to try to grab and uproot a whole tree. It is seemingly impossible, therefore, to grab and uproot those artifacts you have in the mind: those of your religion, those of your society, those things that you call beliefs, those things that are beliefs and you do not understand as such, those that are the beliefs you call science and knowledge, those things that you cherish, those things which you know to be taboo and that are, nevertheless, in this jungle.

You are walking now as if you can appreciate and order those things in the jungle. You are becoming adept at journeying and are congratulating yourself for this astuteness of mind. Perhaps you have little papers say you have graduated from mind stages. And yet, you are only on the second node, as far as we are concerned.

Do not trouble yourself with this dilemma. As regular and ordered as this journey has been, we now lie lurking in the depths of the forest. I am the tiger. I am the second node.

You do not want to face us, yet you feel our presence. You have caught a glimpse of us. You have found our tracks and have seen the remnants of our meal. You are now aware that the tiger can come at any moment into this beautifully oriented, wonderfully symbiotic, fantastically diverse and yet incredibly ordered jungle. We do come, indeed. We are those beings who rip and claw apart, tear out creation around you and devour it. You are afraid of us. Yet, we are terrible and wonderful at the same time to you.

Why are we here? What purpose do we serve? We serve the very purpose of destruction, of tearing and rending. Do you not notice that the denseness of this jungle around you is not bringing you to enlightenment? There are so many shrubs, so many vines, so many trees whose roots have taken hold in the Earth. You need to know that the bark of these tree trunks can be ripped and torn apart. You need to know that the animals which now abound in the creation of this mind are a result of all those other life-forms around it. Those things that have been planted now hold animals. And these animals are feeding on those plants and trees in this jungle. There is life in great density in this jungle, and yet, all of these things need to be able to be destroyed and to be devoured or else this jungle will become impassable.

Knowing this you fear us. You fear that even as we tread upon this soft, moist black soil of the jungle, we may crush the most beautiful plants; we may devour the most brilliant birds. We may even rend apart your very flesh.

You must confront this tiger, however. This tiger is, for you, change. It is the destruction of that which you have valued, or even that for which you have a nostalgia. It is seeming to destroy your past experience, but then, perhaps some little thought is there to tell you that you do not have to lose experience.

Those most cherished thoughts, those highest principles may fall, may be devoured. Those sturdiest trees may have their flesh ripped apart. Your ego, your personality, and you yourself may have your flesh ripped apart. Your notions of God, of nature, of what is true, of what is not true, your ideas that have become so rooted in you, are like living things. They have transmuted themselves. They have crossed that barrier between thought and reality and are now artifacts of the mind. Trees with huge trunks, although they have sprouted forth from your imagination, experience or learning, are now beyond your control. It is our energy which will rend them asunder, for there is nothing in your mind that cannot be ripped apart. It is a terrible thing to say, but as those who journey into the jungle realize, nothing about which they can think is sacred.

What temple has not fallen to men of arms? You know that as a civilizations come and go, ideas in turn come and go with them— ideas about life, the nature of God and of humankind. Likewise, it is our energy that takes from you those things you cherish sometimes to the greatest degree, takes those things which are like a civilization inside you, like your own internalized culture. We take those things from you which are sometimes the most precious, until you realize that all these thoughts are ephemeral. They are not made safe by you. They are not free from time and decay.

There is a point in your journey in which you become resigned to this. You are resigned to life and death. You know that it is part of the natural order that things are destroyed. Surrounding this, you have some sense of wisdom growing inside you. However, we are the tiger and you know that we have power beyond what you see as the natural world. Eventually, in your journey, you become aware that we can overcome you as well as anything and you are afraid for self. It is fine for tiger to take the animals which scurry on the jungle floor or to rip the bark of a tree. It is fine for what you call, in your foolishness, survival of the fittest. It is fine for all these things to take place. It is when tiger stares at you from behind the bushes that you know tiger can take the self. Of all the things that you build up in your mind, all the intellectual thoughts, all the thoughts about relationships, all the thoughts about science and God, the thought of self now seems to be the most imperiled. You are in the greatest fear that the tiger will take a swipe at you, and overwhelm you.

The tiger will destroy self. It is this confrontation, ultimately, which you must have. And, it is the second node. The realization that self is not anymore permanent than anything which is seen out in nature, or than any great, vast civilization which was built centuries and centuries ago, that the self is no more permanent than anything which is under the eyes of God. You see winds blow and the surf rise up and pound against the sand. You see birds fall from the sky. You see trees felled by the force of the machinery of humankind. You see so many changes, and yet, the self wishes to cling to life.

I am also your way out. I am your release. If you cannot allow for the possibility of self to die, to change, we will take it upon us to change it for you, and you know this. The forces that are Divine are many. Often what is created must first spring from what is destroyed. What is destroyed is the beginning of what is created, for God is also God Destroyer. We are as much a vision of God as the bird of paradise. When you see us in our terrible form, you know that you have a sense of awe about God. We represent that to you. We humbly and yet proudly represent that to you.

Be at peace, my friends, with God on this Earth. You will see destruction in your lifetime and wonder what its purpose is. Its purpose is to clear, to release, to make way for a new creation. You must allow self to die and be reborn - to change until you realize that the self is part of the natural world, just like the plants that spring up with beautiful flowers and then die the next season. Self is as much a part of this natural world as the small animals which scurry across the leafy floor of the jungle, seemingly without self-awareness. You do not want the destruction of self, but you must know that something will be created in its ruin. In its death something new will be born.

Be at rest with this. And let us impart our love and our energy to you as we go. Good-bye.

The Orchid

The Third Node

Your journey through the jungle has taken you through much already. If you have been astute and willing to learn, at least two things have happened. You have first encountered the bird of paradise. You have encountered the internal vision of God that is in your mind, the spark within, the spark of your creation, the spark of your enlightenment, the spark of your Divinity. And you realize now at this new stage, this third node, that you have the alternative not to pursue a course through the jungle, not to make this journey, not to be involved in the trials of finding your path through such an intricate place thick with life. And, yet, here you are. You are still journeying and still making progress. This is fine.

A contemplative may have rested at the edge of the forest and have gone no further. But you are not such a being. You are an explorer. Exploration of the mind is most important. Those uncharted territories of the Earth, becoming fewer and fewer in number, tend to make some look to the planets and the stars for exploration and knowledge. But, we know that the depths of the mind are the greatest unexplored territory. They yield the greatest fruit. They have the most profound significance for humankind.

This journey need not have begun, but it has. So at this point, you are at the third node, as we have said. You are aware of the God Light inside you. You have taken the bird of paradise with you. Indeed, the bird has been around you all of the time. You have not forgotten. You have learned and become acculturated to the ways of the jungle. We spoke about order for you. What order there is in your mind, you know can be dismembered—ripped apart by tiger energy. You know that whatever concepts you have about God, about yourself, can be torn asunder. You know that this is as much a creative force as that force of the Mother God who nourishes and protects. But, at this point, in this node, you begin to fashion a new reality. You come to the realization that you have not crossed paths with the tiger, but, that you now are the tiger. You are this force that rips apart, rips you from one place to another, rips concepts out of your mind, rips out things which you cherish, and releases you from the bondage of the mind, of the self. Already you have been born and remade many times in one life. Now, you realize you are the tiger. And the tiger cannot threaten you anymore, because you are he; you are this tiger, so, you are at peace. Is it not in the nature of peace that while you are happiest being peaceful, you also acknowledge the possibility of violence? It is part of the nature of peace that you come to terms with violence.

And so, you meet me. I am a devic being. I am a deva of flowers. Just as the bird of paradise is the most beautiful, most entrancing of all the birds in the jungle, the orchid is the most beautiful of all the flowers in the jungle. The orchid is the most symbolic of the soul. And, I come to you now in order for you to understand what role I play in creation.

The bird was to remind you of the God Light. The tiger was to remind you of the Destructor God. I am here to remind you of the God who is peaceful. I bring the God of Peace. You have journeyed far, as we have said already, and you are now able to contemplate the beauty around you without allowing fear to upset you and take you off center. You now have embraced love, the sight of God, and God's almighty power, you see. You have embraced the tiger and the bird of paradise. You are one with them. You realize that they are you. And, you are now beginning not to worry so much about the order of the jungle, or your ability to cope. You have time now to appreciate the beauty of it. You have time to appreciate the joy. You give attention now to everything of beauty around you: flowers, trees, animals, sky. Their ensemble itself is beautiful. The black earth is beautiful. The orchid is your resting spot now. You sit and watch it in contemplation. It seems to you to be the most beautiful, peaceful thing in the world. Yes, you can sit and your mind can go back to encounters with the tiger and you can yet be at peace with these encounters. There is some thought of fear in you, but there also is some feeling of resignation. There is acceptance for tiger. There is acknowledgment of the bird of paradise, of the God Light within you. In these contemplations, in this meditative state you cease to spin the world around you. You are at rest. The world is at rest. You have focus and concentration. You choose to focus on the most beautiful things of the world. You choose not to focus on ugliness, disaster. It is your choice, and you are making it. You are empowering yourself to see beauty and to see love around you. And, you are using the orchid to do this.

It is a very wonderful step. You feel that you could go on and on forever. But your understanding that you are on a trek through the jungle is not such great knowledge. You contemplate abandoning the journey at this point. Everything seems to have been done already. All the journeys seem to have been made. You are one with nature. What further step do you need to take? Where can you possibly go from here? If you are meant to go to God, then you do not need to take one step forward, and you know it. If you are meant to have a realization, you believe that all realizations can be obtained in beauty. You only have a vague sense of the purpose of this mission, your journey, and you are not really appreciating where you are going and why.

Nevertheless, this obscurity of purpose is overshadowed by light. And, you think that because it is overshadowed by such brilliant, beautiful light, the light coming from this flower, you cannot be wrong. And you are correct. There is no need to go forward from this point unless you truly want to. In your feeling of resignation and acceptance, you begin to contemplate whether it is not the journey's end that is most important, but the fact that you are journeying. You realize that you do not need to know where it is that you are going, but, you need to enjoy what you are doing. You also realize that to continue the journey may be just as worthwhile, just as wonderful as to stay put. You realize that any goal will be altered by every step you take.

It may be that your idea of meditation, your contemplation of peace, may start to expand. It is for a good purpose that you are looking at the orchid. The orchid, as you know, is merely a point of departure. For, as you have internalized all things in the jungle, you are internalizing the orchid and realizing that there truly is no still point, that the still point is really just as active a point as any, and that in internalizing peace, calm, and resignation by observation and contemplation of all the bittersweet beauty around you, you are free to go forward in peace. You are free to move through creation.

Your choices may not be the choices you think. So, why be afraid to choose? You have even thought, "Perhaps, I do not need to choose at all." But that was the beginning of your meditation. Now, you think, "All choosing is the same, and I do not need to be afraid of choosing." You stand up and look ahead. You are still contemplating the orchid. It has seemed to you the only orchid in the universe. Any other knowledge is not necessary. Rather than seek out other places of beauty, other orchids, you take this orchid with you. This is not baggage in your mind; it is not creating heaviness. You are creating lightness, since the orchid has many petals and many aspects. It has no limitation. The orchid is much like a crystal whose facets work with each other to create an echoing energy. You decide to move onward, but the beauty of the orchid is with you.

My friends, I know that you hear my words with love and in contemplation. You feel many times that you want to be in this place, above all. You see, we are simply the third node; we are not the end of this journey. Yet, you savor your moments of peace and meditation, the moments of beauty in your life. You may be matured in the understanding that there are moments of destruction, despair, and turmoil. And yet, this does not impede your appreciation of the beauty and the silence in the jungle, the silence that is with you, inside you. The vision of God is one also of peace, not just of the tiger.

You may wish to linger in this spot. When you do, all the flower essences come to you. And not all flowers have the same fragrance as the orchid. When you wish too much to take in essence from the flower, you begin not to discriminate. It could be the essence of the poppy which you are taking in. It could be that you are becoming inebriated with that flower. This is the trap of the flower essence. It is intoxicating. It can be addictive. Be careful about what you take into your body. If you end up lingering in this spot, you will succumb to addiction. If you succumb to addiction, it will only seem as if this is the still point in your existence, as if this is the spot in which you must rest. It will seem as if you have reached your goal and there is nothing further here to do. This is as much illusion as anything in your world.

I am proud of that beauty which I help the orchid to impart to the world. We are here to serve them. And orchids are here to serve you with their beauty. It is the reason they exist. We know that you cannot understand, entirely, anything of such great beauty. But, remember that nothing about God can be understood in its entirety. The need for contemplation you now realize is over. You are picking yourself up.

Unfetter yourself, my friends, from those addictions, those intoxications in life, and move onward. We have blessings, for you and all of your kind.

We thank you.

The Fourth Node

Welcome. You have now come to the fourth node. This node is something of a mystery to you. You do not know yet that it exists. And many of you do not understand the implications in something which can become so apparent and, at the same time, remain most mysterious.

I am the being from whom you least wish to hear at this point. I am the being that inspires a type of fear that is different from that of the tiger. You are afraid to confront something when you see me. And yet, here I am, suddenly standing in front of you in this jungle. The next stage in your journey is that of confrontation. The confrontation is with humanity. I am the village chief.

You have entered into a village. You did not believe that there were any other people alive in the forest. You did not believe that people thrived in this place which seemed so foreign and hostile to you. You have made efforts to conquer all those aspects of the jungle you believed were savage, untamed—those things which wanted to bring you harm or of which you are afraid. But, we are here flourishing in that very same jungle which was such a struggle for you to subdue.

But your mind is never in need of being subdued. Your mind is not to be conquered. Your mind is not to be disciplined, or to be directed. It is not energy to be harnessed. It is, instead, a rich thing, full of life, full of joy.

You may want to go far away from the village now that you have been here. Your feelings say to you, "I am not comfortable now. I am not sure if this is a hostile greeting or if this is a friendly greeting. Who are these natives of the jungle?" You are afraid to know.

We consider you natives also, my friends. So, why is there fear in your confrontation? It is because you have flattered yourself that you have taken this journey alone, that there is no one who has done it before you. You have propped yourself up. You were the mighty explorer. Your wit, your bravery and your skill had gotten you far into the jungle where no one had been before. And yet, here in front of you there is a village chief—myself. Behind me there is a whole village full of people doing everything you can imagine right in the midst of the forest.

You only know that you have penetrated the densest part of the jungle, my friends, when you confront me. This fear that you have is not the fear of being alone. It is the fear of not being alone. This fear you have is the fear that I will reveal something about your own humanity, that I will share with you your own humanity, that I will laugh and joke with you about it. It is not just the representation that is so fearful to you, although this is fearful enough in itself. I do represent humanity, but I also represent your humanity. I represent all other paths which you now understand take you to the same place. For your path through the jungle has taken you to the same place where my people live, and you are not comfortable with that. But, it is not even this fear that is the greatest fear inside you.

The greatest fear inside you now is the fear that I will begin to communicate. It was not fear that we will not be able to communicate, it is the fear that we will. And, this fear that you will be able to dialogue with me tells you that your defenses will have to be brought down. The sense of self will have to perish, because of what there is now to communicate. Step by step, in the process of communication, we must learn and relearn about our own humanity. We must bring to mind those things we share in common. You need to eat. You need a place to sleep. Perhaps you desire a woman or a man. Perhaps you are in need of some guidance or skill. Perhaps there is something you want to share. Perhaps you are ill and want healing. All these things are reminders of your own humanity. There is no way to communicate to another human without having that communication be an affirmation of your own and their own humanity. Anything else would dehumanize the other and would not be true communication.

So, this barrier now needs to be breached. You are not form-ing a bridge to another world with this communication. You are sim-ply acknowledging your own humanity. We are, after all, in the dens-est part of the forest. This almost impenetrable jungle is not the world and is not meant to represent the world. It represents you. You are such a village being. This journey, which you have taken in the mind, has brought you to this point, this confrontation of your own human-ity.

Indeed, as you walk about, you see we do our daily tasks. Our hunters go out in the morning into the jungle and come back into the village in the evening. The women do their chores. The children play. The elders teach. People build houses. They make pots. They plow fields. They plant. You see all these things. You see yourself reflected in all these labors. We are you. Let us say, for the sake of the mind, we are your memory. We are a memory which stretches far back into time. We are the memory of all the details of your life that you have wanted to put aside for your ideals—the cleaning, the cooking, the chores, the building, the destruction, what you call work, the care of a family, learning and teaching. Since you have taken up your jour-ney, you have believed that all these things have been left behind for the pursuit of lofty ambitions, but now you find them right here in the heart of the jungle. This is now where you know your attention must turn. You have come across three stages, after all, three nodes. This fourth node is daily life. You are aware at this time that you cannot make a separation between your loftiest thoughts, your great-est ambitions, your spiritual drive, and the routine needs and wants of your life.

What is more annoying is that when we do these things, we are somehow touched by grace, that there is sacredness in our every-day activities. This is not far from reality, my friends. For, those people whom you believe to be the most primitive in this world, have been able to be constant in the knowledge of the sacredness of every small prosaic act, every daily routine. When we are mirroring this to you, we also mirror a glorified humanity, a sacred humanity, the Human God. You can, in this node, begin to see its sacredness in the coarseness and the mundaneness of everyday life. But, you first must begin to communicate. Your communication must be deep and strong, and must be true and fervent. You must embrace those ordinary things which you have believed to be impediments distracting you from the spiritual dreams that you have had. You must take and embrace those things, love them, and show them to yourself anew.

My friends, as much as you fear our first encounter, it is only possible to go further. You could destroy us because we remind you too much of those things that you wish to deny in your own self. It is true that in the process of colonization many such villages have been destroyed. But it is easier for the lone traveler to create welcome for themselves, and to begin to dialogue with that part of their humanity which they would not admit was there.

There is a sacredness in everything that you do. There is as much joy in the turning of a potter's wheel as there is in the turning of the Earth creating day and night. There is as lofty an ambition in one healing prayer as there is in creating peace between nations. There is no great difference, my friends, between any two hearts and two minds. We ask for you to be welcome. We are willing to share. We feel that you will respond in love and we are happy. We rejoice. And you find acceptance in us.

So, we ask that this inner journey bring you self-acceptance. It is possible. It is likely. You are surrounded, and so have not much of a choice, since you are, after all, outnumbered. You are in the midst of it. You can be overwhelmed by it, or you can find acceptance of your own humanity.

We thank you.

The Fifth Node

W elcome to the fifth node. It has been your secret desire to see me. You have not let the words pass from your lips, and yet, we see your heart and we know that your desire to see us has been great. You have had, perhaps, a professed desire to confront the tiger. Tiger has taught you non-attachment. However, this non-attachment has been to those things of self, which you have seen around you in nature. You now must learn a different form of non-attachment, and you seek me out subconsciously. I am here and I heal. I heal in this village. I am the shaman. People come to me for healing, and much like a broken record, I have the same response to all of them: "If it is you who must heal," I say, "you must heal yourself."

You are sitting down. We are having a ceremony in this village. This ceremony is one of much noise. There is a great fire burning in the center of a circle, for the people of your village are gathered in a circle around this fire. Drums are beating, or people are beating drums. And, you now are not sure which. There is chanting and singing that echo through the jungle, or there is chanting and singing that emanate from the bowels of the forest itself. You are, likewise, not sure of this. A strange ritual is being performed, the nature of which you are not certain, or you already know this ritual from time out of mind. It is night time. The stars shine, but the smoke from the fire sometimes obscures this light. You have only been adopted by this village, and yet you feel at one with it.

I am shaking a rattle and singing. You recognize me now as the healer of your mind, of your self. As the ritual goes on, the beating of the drums becomes more forceful. Energy seems to percolate upwards from the root of your being and seems to be calling you to ecstasy. It seems to be calling forth rapture and raw feeling. And it is.

You begin to remember and to realize something. You have journeyed far, so you think. You have journeyed through many experiences already.

There was a time you can remember in which you saw yourself very differently. Now, through these many nodes, you find yourself in the fire, in the node of the shaman. You realize, first, that you have changed so much you would not recognize yourself now if you saw yourself with the eyes of the person you were many years ago. You see, instead, someone new, someone transformed. And yet, the fire burns, and burns this new one away even as you think it.

You finally begin to realize that you are insane, that you have held in attachment those things called self, one after another. Like someone who has clawed their way through the jungle, you have clutched one idea of self after another. But, at this point, you are realizing that all ideas of self are equally insane. This energy coming up from your root tells you that it is more powerful than anything else, that it is overwhelming any sense of self you have, any clinging to self you want. This root energy is calling up something greater than self.

This is the power of God, the God of Ecstasy welling up inside you. It is the power of passion that causes creation. It is the power of passion that causes destruction. You realize that any clinging, any attachment to self, is insanity. And, as I shake my rattle, you see that I am telling you this must be true. You have been living in a state of psychosis all your life. You have been given opportunity after opportunity to recognize this, and now you are burning this insanity in the fire at last. This is the fifth node, the node of no self.

If you depart the fifth node, you come to a realization that the journey is no longer important. It is the traveler who is important. And, you are this traveler, of course. You must proceed onward now with this knowledge that there has been no need to journey, that there has not been a journey. If you do not, then you will be lost and you know it. You have a thought and a vision of home. And, this memory is what guides you now.

Thank you.

The Sixth Node

My friends, the sixth node is no node, and it is all nodes at the same time. The sixth node is a transcendent state and it is the state of great immersion in life.

You have left your ritual. You have realized that there is inside you a great need to go home. For whatever purpose you have undertaken this journey, you have realized now that you are this journey, and that it did not matter. You realize that you have become the journey and the journey has become nothing. You wish simply to go back home; although, the memory of home is very frail. You have little recollection of that place and time. Your first duty, therefore, is to hire a guide. And, you are attempting now to discover which guidance will best take you home. It could be another soul. It could be a thought form. In the same way a compass directs you, the magnetism of thought can direct you. It could be a message you are receiving in the village, directions from those you respect—the shaman, or the village chief. But, you know that you need guidance, and you take it.

You embark on your new journey, the journey back home. In this journey you do not count the days, and you do not worry about those aspects of the jungle which you have already encountered— the tiger, or the orchid, or the bird. You do not worry about encountering the snake or crossing the stream or climbing the rock. You are not counting days, but still you feel that you are going on a journey of great importance.

So, you do not know how many days you have travelled when you find yourself in the middle of the night by your own small fire. And, suddenly, you become aware that whomever you hired to take you out of the jungle—for you have hired someone as a guide—has left you and you are entirely alone. You sit by the fire and you think, "Why do I fear? I have gone beyond merely conquering the jungle; I am now at one with it. There is nothing the jungle can present to me which will cause me to fear—snake, tiger, rain storm—nothing." And yet, there is a stirring inside that there is something amiss, that all throughout this time, all throughout the other nodes, you have been lacking something which you did not understand. You may believe that you have abandoned self and embraced something higher. Or, you may be in a new self, which in turn will die to another. Whatever the case is, you understand in your fear that there is something more. What is it?

You are on the verge of uttering the words to yourself, and yet, you realize that you need courage to do so. Sitting by your own fire that burns so brightly and boldly, you cannot help but let them slip out of your mouth. You speak your realization. "I am the Creator God."

It is you who has created your journey. It is you who has created the nodes—the tiger, the bird, the orchid, the village. It has all been your creation. There is a tingling that goes up the spine when you think of it.

You are at once in awe and at peace. You are charged with fire. You are content and resigned. Your soul has partaken of God-Essence, and now the Creator God is the condition of your humanity. It is a wonderful and an earth-shaking realization.

It is not that you have transcended this jungle and your journey. It is not that you have not. It is that you have created them. You now know, alone in this forest teeming with life, which you cannot see in the darkness, that you must create what it is you most desire as the sun rises. You must manifest from the mind who you wish to be. You must end the dichotomy between the one who experiences, and the experience itself. You must stop creating this duality between who is and who acts. You must cease your thought that self is different, that self can be distinguished from its surroundings. It cannot. As the sun rises in the sky, you realize that you must create what the light of the sun illuminates, the light whose genesis was God. Whatever the sun makes manifest is to be yours. You must create it.

You, being this great Creator God, have but one responsibility to this creation. And, unless you honor it, you know that you are doomed. Unless you begin to create and respond, you are doomed.

What is the response of a God to their creation? The only response is love. It is love that you must manifest on this Earth and before the sunrise. There must be a manifestation of great love, or else you know that you are doomed.

I am the Archangel Ezekiel. I bid you welcome from all the realms beyond sight and beyond the universe you know. We are as one with you in this. Our responsibility is also one of love, for we are creation, and we are the Creator. The freedom to act, my friends, is the freedom of love. The freedom to respond is the freedom to love. Know that as that divine spark is in you, you ignite the fires of creation with it, becoming the Creator yourself. Heed my warning: as you open your eyes and you go about the work of the world, there is nothing which you should not love.

In your pursuit of God, in your journey, you have formed conceptions of what is true for you. Your command now to love comes from God. This command to love requires that you love everything, truth and untruth. And, while you have discarded self, you have also discarded truth as untruth. You have discovered that some things you have held as truth are now untruth. At this juncture you are working with the deepest and darkest places inside you to bring them out into light. Just as you are seated in the midst of the night forest where there are no stars above you, a night sky which is occluded and black, and just as you know that the morning will bring a new creation, you realize that the mind, in holding the difference between truth and untruth, is in darkness. You need to realize that untruth has been guiding you as much as you believe truth has. You must embrace untruth in love, for you have been learning from it. You have been using it as guidance. And, you must offer it up to the fire. You can begin to see, when you embrace this untruth, that everything which has gone before has been annihilated. You have destroyed everything in your acceptance of untruth in your life. And, from that point, your attention is now firmly fixed on your own manifestation. For has not what you have thought of as truth been something which has been injected into your reality? It has been adopted. It has, in fact, been the truth of others which you have most closely kept and cherished next to your heart.

And now, you begin to see that what you have created around you is you. The dawn will rise; this new day must be yours. Do not be afraid to take this step. It is a natural step—one in which you must understand and comprehend that all is yours.

And so, this is your moment of contemplation and determination. The last part of the mind with which you want to contend is the darkest part of your mind. It was not dark with the tiger. It was not dark with the fierce tribal warriors. It was dark with yourself, alone. It is the darkest part of you. This part, like untruth, like falsehood, like emptiness, demands that you do something, that you create.

You may be able to create out of untruth better than you can create out of truth. Truth is intrusive. Truth is already fabricated whenever you identify truth as outside of yourself. It is its own manifestation; it is creation already brought to pass. That truth outside of yourself is ultimately, untruth. But you cannot see this yet. You first must reach this point of greatest darkness.

In this world, in this time, creativity in love is the most precious thing. If you are not happy with untruth, use it to create something. We give this to you as a warning, because life is not going to be sustained in this realm very long, if you do not begin to create. You have been stifling this urge to create, because you believe that you must be the master of the jungle, to face this or that, or understand this or that. In reality, what you needed to do was to create. Anything that you saw, ultimately, was untruth, because it did not come from you. It was not creation from you.

Unless you begin to create, all will be lost upon this Earth. Anything else that you do is of little significance. Any other node is insignificant, once you reach the sixth node. You can draw upon it for experience or you can let it go. We do not care. Once you reach the sixth node, you realize that the sixth node is the only node. You cannot be there and be anywhere else at the same time. Once you get to the sixth node, you cannot have passed through the other five nodes. You are simply in it.

When the dawn arises on this Earth, you had better create what you need to create. And the dawn is now arising. If you find that you have not created it, what will happen? You will be in a false node and you will be swept away by creation. The plants will become toxic and will burn your skin. The Earth will swallow you up. The animals will pick at your flesh. You have absolutely nothing else to do at this time but create. If you choose to do anything else, you will be destroyed.

It is time for you to create. Now, you must decide whether you want to create and live, or to die. The sixth node is creation. But, that is what the jungle was, creation teeming with life. You are the Creator-God. You have been looking at creation in such complexity, variety, exultation and unbelievable vigor, and yet, you have not taken the hint that all throughout this time you were supposed to be creating spontaneously. Where else but in a jungle were you to learn this? You are in the midst of great creation, but it is not yet your creation.

We say, unless you love God, you will die. Now, unless you create, you will not love. You cannot create anything which is not out of love. So, unless you create, you will die. Are you worried, distressed about what is happening in your world and society? These are not your creations. What do you care? They are untruths to you. It is time for you to create, for you to ignore them.

You have no nodes left. The sixth node is the destruction of all other nodes. Unless you begin to create, you will be swept away by unreality, falsehood, your own psychosis, the creation of others—whatever you wish to call it. Unless you begin to create, all will be lost. And so, we give you this parting warning: this is the time, my friends, to move.

I will say something more to you. Creation is taking place on a false level; there is a parallel node which is destructive. Unless you are willing to accept that sixth node, you will suffer, because more falsehood is created than truth in this world. Creation is taking form, and manifestation is going to be one way or the other. God will devour false creation. If you do not manifest your truth, God will devour your untruth, and, in the meantime, you will be devoured with it. The last part of your self is the part that is the creative self which does not want to be put to work. Please grasp this.

This is the end of your journey through the jungle, and you no longer care anymore what has transpired. The sixth node is your creativity. Please embrace it now before it is too late.

Thank you.

Book Two

Part One

Compassion

Preface

As we pass through the six nodes, the responsibility we have in love becomes that of action, that of being willing to surrender to experience. So, now are called upon the six gates of compassion. You are welcome here. You are capable of understanding these gates beyond their context in the whole.

But, we want you to know that these entities, who will come to you to present each of the six gates, were carefully chosen to be as diverse and yet as appropriate as possible. Remember that they are the best living representations of the nature and the purpose of the gates.

We cannot take you through another journey. But, we can take you through these gates. As opposed to the nodes, it is not possible for you to be fixed in any one gate at a time. You must pass through these gates in sequence, the gates being like movements of a dance. And this will become apparent as you are reading. However, you may be struggling in your life with any one of these gates. Please be aware of what we say. One is not more important than the other. At the time you are struggling it may seem so, but one cannot be more important than the other.

Your passage through these gates is a journey back to the Godhead. We wish you love and blessings from that Source.

The Sea Otter

The First Gate

I appreciate you as friends and, as a friend, I wish to share with you the experiences of my life. I am here to represent the first gate. The first gate is one of great joy. And, indeed, we move ourselves with great joy as if energy just springs from our root, like fireworks. We are beings with wonderfully flexible spines who move with great fluidity and speed and great exhilaration throughout the land and water. I am not a deva, but a being who is alive, someplace on this Earth right now. As you are picking up this book and reading it, know that I am at play somewhere in the world. Indeed, the first gate is one of joy, play, creativity, and exuberance, of raising your energy up from the bottom. It is my task today to share with you my experience with this gate.

I am an otter, a sea otter, for you are here at the seashore wanting to embark on the world of experience. You know the difference between you and me is that I seem to be freer than you. No one is telling me to go to work. No one is showing me the responsibilities I have towards my family. No one is trying to discipline my mind. I do not give credence to ideologies. I am not socialized, at least not in the human way. Although we have a wonderful society, it is not one where I feel the strain of duty or the burden of social responsibility. When you encounter us, you become a little bit jealous. Why? Let us take a look at how this is true.

Our freedom is but one component of us. You know that we are at home both at sea and on land. You also are aware that we are at play. And, indeed, we do things solely for the purpose of creative play and not for the purpose of merely feeding ourselves. The mistake that humans could make in looking at animals is believing that our lives are bound up in survival. Over and over again, you must hear messages to the contrary. Eventually, it will sink in. You are learning, too, as a species, and it takes a while for you, in the same way it takes us some time to learn.

In our play we attain knowledge without effort. This gate is a gate of wisdom without effort. It is the gate, as we said, of creative play. What is different about learning through creative play? Learning has been taught to you as something very passive—to read a book, to study, to absorb the knowledge of another, to deduce a problem, to work out something logically. This is a very passive thing. When you are engaged in play, you relate to your environment immediately. You do not sit in abstract thought. And yet, wisdom comes to you in this manner out of your experience. Learning foisted on you by books is somehow brittle and stale. Some of you may enjoy this stale, overdone, leftover quality of knowledge and wisdom that you get from books, but it really does serve a better purpose to engage in the experience of play.

There is no time in which experience becomes passive. It is not necessary to step back in order to see the big picture. It is not necessary to detach yourself in order to grow in wisdom. In fact, as you have your own visceral, immediate experience, it is imperative that you do not step back. It is important that you do not try to detach yourself, because this is a game of the mind and not reality. You can never detach yourself from your own experience. The best thing you can do in relationship to your experience is to be willing to be playful and active in terms of it, to be willing to engage in experience. Know that whatever you think is happening to you, is happening with you—you are engaged. You are neither doing it nor is it happening to you. You are experiencing it. You are with life. These separations, which you believe are possible, between thought and deed or between passivity and activity, are false dualities.

In the search for your God Essence, you believe yourself to be working actively, but internally. We can say to you that your work, which appears to be external, which is your work in relationship to the world or the realm of experience, equally drives you into your own God Essence. You cannot go inward and then yank out an enlightened self to be at play in the world. You must first be willing to engage the world in play as an enlightened being and be willing to acknowledge your engagement as you are now. You cannot hope to put one before the other. You cannot go inward and then decide to be outward. You must be at one with all that you are: that being who is worldly, who is experiencing, for whom there are others in the world, and that being for whom the God Light burns inside, for whom there is a soul that exists regardless of all other souls, who is loved by God regardless of whether anyone else can be loved by God. This is your nature.

In the realm of the animals we do not pretend to seek perfection. The human realm seeks perfection at all times, sanctifies its search for perfection, and, in the process, diminishes the realm of experience. You then begin to call yourselves sinners in some way or another. We suggest you take a look at your society, your religions, and ask yourselves why you would ever call yourselves sinners. Would you do better to substitute another word? You may not want to feel guilty of sin, so you may declare that you can make an error or a mistake. But, you are in reality merely substituting words when you say this.

What we wish to impart to you now is that you need to see yourself in experience without judgment, and you need not to wait for the time of purification to act. In the realm of the animals, we do not judge ourselves as being so imperfect that we cannot engage ourselves in one activity over another. If it seems as if we can, we make an attempt. Of course I cannot fly—the character in the next gate will fly. My attempt would be foolish. I could make it, but then I would learn that flying is not for me. But, I can swim. And, I can walk on land, and run as well. You might say to me, "For those who run on land, swimming is not for them. For those who swim, they should not try to run on land." But, we want to say, "If you can do it, you need to be engaged in it." I say this without moralizing. For, is it possible for you to pick up a gun, for instance, and murder another? You will say, "No otter, this is not possible for me." And, I bow to that in you. Understand what I am saying, and that I am not speaking necessarily about moving the physical body—that was simply an analogy. If it is truly possible for you to do it, you were meant to experience it in some way at some time.

Your movement through experience is just as holy as all those inner ideals to which you hold so fast. Begin this part of acceptance and non-judgment of yourself, and allow yourself to engage in play. Remember that you are always active—you cannot go through the world feeling passive, feeling as if things are happening to you. The only thing that you can truly call experience is something with which you are one, not something which is happening to another, not something which is happening to you, not something which you are doing, and not something which someone is doing to you. It is something with which you are together.

Watch our bodies as we move through the sea. We are with the water and the tidal forces. We are with the terrain as we leap and slide about the Earth. We are with. At some time in this gate, you will begin to understand that there is no difference between what is done and who is doing it. There is no difference between who is the doer and the receiver. You can only be engaged in experience. You cannot dominate it, nor can it dominate you. If you ask yourself why things are happening to you, you are not at play. If you ask yourself why you did something, you are, likewise, not at play. Do not feel as if things happen to you. And, please, do not feel as if you are doing things. You are at play. You are one with experience.

This is our wisdom. The next gates will present to you something more because we are not sufficient in and of ourselves. My gate does not stand alone. And, every gate opens up to a vast playing field. You are standing now on the sea strand. The sand pebbles beneath your feet are gray, and the water is lapping at this shore. And you see the ocean spread out in front of you. The next entity will wish to give you a vision of that ocean.

Thank you.

The Owl

● The Second Gate

H ello. I am he who comes to you as the second gate. Will you stand at the shore and look out towards the ocean? Your gaze goes up. You see me above you and beyond you, for I am flying over the part of the seacoast on which your feet are planted. I look with knowing upon what you look with longing. The second gate which I represent to you is one of vision, of discernment, one of experience through seeing, of wisdom through intuition and insight. So important is sight to us that our eyes are incredibly large and we see at night as well as day.

I am owl. You have some jealousy again for us. We do things which are unimaginable to you. If we seem to you not to enjoy or partake in our own experience, you are mistaken. We have knowledge of self, and so we know who enjoys. We are one who is enjoying, who is experiencing.

You wish your self to take steps to cross the ocean, perhaps to get to a foreign place. You wish, perhaps, to know which steps must be taken, what direction you must go. We have no such difficulties where we are, soaring above you. Our eyesight is so great that the whole world is laid out in front of us. If we wish to find our prey below us, we can pluck it out from its environment readily.

As vast as this world is, and as vast as your range of experience is in it, you must know that you need to focus attention, to have the insight to reach your goal. We give you this warning: you must not allow your vision to be overwhelmed by experience. You must allow yourself, at once, to see the landscape before you for what it is, and to focus your attention on what you desire. You cannot swoop down swiftly, unless you have first caught your goal in sight.

My friends, if it runs away from you, it is not for you to take. There will be other things on which your attention can focus for the sake of your ambitions. This gate of experience tells you that you must use your mind, use your insight to discern. This gate tells you that you must engage the world of sight as part of experience.

I will give you the most important example. You see a world you have tried to characterize —perhaps, a world of evil, of turmoil, of pollution, of social ills, or, perhaps, a world of people trying to achieve happiness, a world of love. All of the time you are trying to describe the world, your vision is on the whole world. It is as if we were to look over the vast plains and seas over which we fly and not be able to focus on that which we want. It would seem just as confusing to us as it would be to you if we would continue to make judgments of the world as a whole. You need to understand that in spite of all the infinite detail to which we can give our attention, despite all the hurly-burly of the world, we find what we want, having focused our attention on it.

You need this insight yourself. The world will not be changed by your judgment of it. The world is only changed by your experience of it, your willingness to create in it. The more you unfocus your attention, the less you will live with purpose. You will believe yourself to be an astute judge of humankind. You will believe yourself to be a worldly person. You will know the evils of the world and, perhaps, its good parts. But, you will not be able to get at what you want. You will not be able to claim yourself as Creator Gods. Every time you look to define the world in which you live, you surrender an aspect of yourself to chaos. The more you focus on what you desire, the greater your ability to create in this world. And, since this is so, why belabor your problems? Have the insight, rather, to look closely at yourself and at what you are engaged in, to pick out what you want, to grasp onto it, and to make it yours. In the second gate, the gate of insight, this knowing must be with you always.

We can look within or without. We know that you will accept the idea that there is no difference between the two. We could well turn our attention within, sit perched above all others, preen, and contemplate ourselves. But, our demands are such that we wish to fly outward from this inner point, because we trust that we are these Creators ourselves and can find what we need in creation. The first thing you always do find is what you need. It is the first thing that you always create. But, it is the easiest thing to overlook.

How small is our prey? It is quite small. It is small compared to that endless landscape over which we are flying. And yet, we are able to pick it out. The first thing you create as God is what you most need for yourselves. This is sometimes the most difficult thing on which to focus, and to seize.

You are jealous of us. I do not blame you. However, our grandeur does not lie in the strength of our great eyes. It is in our willingness to be one with our experience, to use those things that were given to us, which we found within ourselves—those things you call our attributes. The attribute of which you are most envious, is our skill in navigating through the skies at night. Your minds interpret what we do as seeing through darkness. And yet, we see no darkness, do we? For, it is only light that can be seen. My friends, let this be your principle guidance in the world. Let your goals be fixed upon only light. Let there be within you, firmly and deeply, the knowledge that there is only light to see, that the act of seeing is the act of recognition of God's Light, that the act of intuition, the search for wisdom through insight, is the realization of God Light. Let yourselves not forget this. Even though you believe yourselves to be in the deepest and darkest places of the soul, let your vision awaken you to the light that is there, for this is what vision does. We can see only light.

Do not lose sight of your goals. Thank you.

The Third Gate

M y friends, I bring you greetings. We are alive. We are dancing at the entrance to the third gate. I am a devic being whose purpose is to work with those small creatures whom you see in the waters beneath your boat. We fish are remarkable beings, if I must say so myself. We live in a sea of wonder. We are painted radiant colors. We live in blue waters and stir them with our beautiful bodies, moving by graceful motion in ensemble with other fish in our school. We are truly wonderful beings.

The gate on which you are now signifies one thing and one thing only. It is silence. Who can better represent silence than we, for when was the last time a fish spoke to you?

Why do you seek silence in experience? Do you wish to attain passivity?

No, you cannot attain this. You would not want it, and we would not violate the words of otter. Would you want to retreat into meditation, to go within the mind? This, after all, is experience. And yet, it is not that of which we speak. Silence is all around you and is part of you. This deep silence is not one of contemplation and meditation, in and of itself. It is one of acknowledging what is between creation and the response of the world to creation.

Between that which does and that which receives, between the wish and the fulfillment, between the trial and the outcome, there falls a silence. This silence does not get extinguished by action or reaction, by deed or consequence. It is simply there. You see at least its potential in all things. It is the emptiness, the emptiness of what is occurring. It is this transcendent emptiness that is silence.

You ask me, "What is it that the silence serves? Why should there be emptiness when there is no duality?" Emptiness is the possibility of all things unrealized. Emptiness is that pause between words. Emptiness is that half a beat of rest before the music begins, which you hear just as clearly as all the wonderful melodies in the symphony. It is the wonder of God's creation, universal and at one with the moment you are in. All silence exists simultaneously, and your experience of it is an experience of its entirety.

Who better than the fish to express silence to you? There are subtle noises all throughout the ocean. We do not speak of what is heard or unheard. For what is heard can stand in silence just as well as no sound at all. We speak about our own voices, which is to say our voices are nonexistent. We, ourselves, maintain silence. We do not cry out. We do not exclaim in joy. We respond silently. We receive in silence. We create in silence.

What does silence do? At the moment you begin to play in this, your creation, and begin to use your wisdom and your vision, you must encounter silence. It is the pause between your creation and your response to that which is created. It is what enables you to hear, because there is no bantering impeding you. There is no grieving or joy being proclaimed by you. You are silent so you can hear the response of creation to its God, so you can hear the response of matter to energy. This is the gift of the fish.

What is going to happen as a result? You, this Creator God, go forward in your playful manner, using your great wisdom, to bring forth creation in the world. But, creation is ongoing, and you must respond even to what you create. Your ability to speak must be tempered by your ability to hear. In this way you can create dialogue between you and what you have created. And, you will see that what you are and what you create are one and the same. But, at the same time, you cannot do anything without establishing a dialogue, one most favorable to you, a dialogue which is the means to enable motion back and forth.

We, who swim in the sea, often swim in schools. The beauty of our movement is made even greater by the multitudes in which we move. In our schools we have a necessity to use silence, since it is silence that enables us to hear, to feel the movement of the other fish in response to our own movement. We are not curtailing play, but we are creating dialogue. We do not stop the movement of our dance. You would have no reason to admire us if we stopped and tried to work out on paper the response of all other fish in our school. This would be an impossible thing to do. However, we can do this moving in play. We enable ourselves, therefore, not just to move and to respond, but to be one with our activity and our perception. At the same time in which we are moving in play, we create the movements of the school.

Your dialogue with your own creation would be stopped if you did not believe that you are constantly at play, creating and recreating. It will stop if you do not believe that what you see is what you have created. And, it needs to speak to you to tell you what it is, to tell you what is going on. It needs to speak to you, and you need to hear it. If you do not open this listening center, you will cease being in your creativity.

This silence is not the silence of the vast world; it is the silence of the soul. In all things, the potential for silence rings like a bell. It rings like a bell, not in hollow notes, but in the resonance of concentric circles. No matter how deeply furrowed are the circles, there is emptiness inside. No matter how resonant is the sound you are hearing, you are also hearing its emptiness. In this emptiness, then, your true continued response to creation contains the potential for all things to exist. Beyond this there can be nothing.

My purpose in being with you is to impart this knowledge of silence. This is only the love we have of our own silence, our own ability to respond to what we know we have made.

The rocks speak, the coral speaks, all the sea creatures speak, the waves speak, and the sunlight speaks. All creation is speaking. Are you listening?

When you feel as if you can no longer obtain guidance in the world, you are at the third gate. The only recourse you have at this point is to allow yourself to be in silence to hear what is constantly being said to you. Hear how creation responds to its God. Hear what you have created.

This third gate demands that you go within and feel, and demands that you cease limiting creation by your lack of acknowledgment of all the possibilities which now exist simultaneously.

We have exhausted our ability to speak, and our purpose in speaking is complete. The fourth gate awaits you in all its power and majesty. We bid you good-bye.

The Fourth Gate

B eyond all other purposes, I am present for the purpose of shedding enlightenment on your own personal power. You have
approached the fourth gate, and I stand near its post and hold
it open for you. I am an entity whose name is Raphael, and I am of
the angelic realm. Here you are. You have gone this far, and yet, the
fourth gate is one that is very intimidating.

You believe the angelic beings have no trouble in crossing
this fourth gate—but you are not such a being. And, it is a mistake
for you to allow your sense of self and your personal power to be
diminished by those whom you believe have greater power and are
closer to God. Since power and energy are yours in some form, you
are afraid that you will misuse power like many of the entities you
have seen in your world. And, you hesitate to pass through this gate
because you know the responsibility can be very great. And it can.
Yet, you know that if you do not move through this gate and begin to
exercise your own power and self-determination, you will be lost in
this world.

We are not speaking to you from on high; only God is truly
enthroned on high. We stand with you and we touch you so that you
can feel our potency and feel the vibration of our luminous body and
feel the nature of its empowerment as you go about those things you
do in the world.

This fourth gate is your response to what you have already
created. It is your ongoing response to what you have created in play.
It is play itself in the form of response. It is creativity itself in the
form of ongoing creativity, creativity in a continuum. It is time for

you to enliven your energetic field, to get energy moving through your bodies, to become energy yourself.

The use of energy to fulfill your destiny and to empower you is all our province. We aid in everything you do. We aid in maintaining, increasing, and improving this flow of energy through you. We understand that you will try to deny this force because it seems to be given to you by us. But, we are simply leading you in your own path, in the same way a guide leads you through a jungle. You follow the guide, not because his goals are your goals. You have, rather, dictated to him your goals. You follow this guide through the jungle because you know that, in imitation of him, you will gain knowledge, you will make your way through experience with strength and with authority, and you will get to where you want to go. But, it is only you who will ultimately reach the destination. The guide has no destination; there is only yours.

We, those angelic beings whom you see as your guides, in the same way, do not tell you where to go and do not maintain creation on your behalf around you. You are the being who creates. We help you only to revitalize yourselves. We help you feed yourselves energy. The fourth gate is one of nourishment and succor. It is one of being provided for, but being provided that raw material of creation which comes from the God Source, not from us. It is your place to make use of this energy, to put one foot in front of another, to create and recreate all of the time. We are not here to do this for you. We are here simply for you to see how one being responds to a creation in the midst of creating it, in the same way your guide in the jungle moves to show you what it is like to move—so that you can learn.

As a being of Light who does not wish darkness to be around, you also wish the paths in your life to be sure and to be clear. All this is possible to an extent, but, my friends, be forewarned that your ability to tread with absolute safety and security through this world of yours is not guaranteed. You have not made a contract with God about this. Your position in heaven, likewise, is not guaranteed, for you cannot make this kind of contract with God. When you work through the complexities of your own creation, you realize, of course, that this contract needed to be made with you, yourself. You cannot guarantee that this contract can be made at all or that the contract will be impervious to tampering. Your choices may very well create stumbling. There may be many hardships along your path. But, we believe you can cope with whatever you create. You can sustain this energy in you needed to continue forward.

We ask you whether you notice any hesitation in the way we speak or the way we act, and if the response is no, and if this raises some envy for myself and others of the angelic realm, I say to stop and listen. We do not gather around you to mock you or to show you what you cannot possibly attain or to present a false goal to you. We come to you so that you can perceive what we show you as your own nature in reflection. We are beings of vast energy. Like the guide who is taking you through the forest, each one of our footsteps taking us forward is full of our own inner power, is certain and secure. We are secure, but not in the idea that we will not have hardships on our journey. We are secure in our own feeling of self empowerment or a feeling that we can draw as much energy as we need from God, in order to do that which we set out to do in this world. The confidence with which we speak to you, and which you feel we have inherently within us, is something deep within you, which needs to be awakened. For how else can you proceed in this creation other than with the greatest confidence?

Where does the source of this creation lie? It lies within you. Where does the source of your experience lie? It lies deep within you. It is this point of origin whose power you need to tap. You need to respond to the world which you have created from the same center that created it. God, from the essence of Being, has created in love. God's response to creation is always love, such that you cannot see where creation has begun or will end because of this wellspring of love from the Godhead, from God Herself. Likewise, you, as God walking upon this Earth, can respond in greatest confidence, because you respond in love. You can respond with the greatest force, because you can respond in love. You can be resilient and indomitable. Your footsteps can go so firmly one after another that you marvel at your own abilities. Allow yourself to know that this is an imperative. It is impossible to go forward without confidence, since you are the genesis of all your experience.

We do not hover high above you, my friends. For, outside this realm of the Earth, there is only the blackness of space. We would be huddling in the darkness. If we are here amongst you, do we feel uncomfortable on the soil of the Earth? We most certainly do not feel uncomfortable in any creation, because we know that this is also our creation. And, we do not feel above and beyond you.

Take our hand if you are feeling that you cannot go forward. Take our hand and we will guide you. As you feel our strength and our energy, this will awaken your own. Your strength and energy will course through your body like new blood. When you feel as if you cannot go on, remember that it is you who has created, and only you who can respond. You cannot create anything beyond yourself. You cannot create anything with which you cannot cope. You cannot create any beauty, joy, or love that you cannot hold within you. If something is lost, you can wish it back again. If darkness seems to descend, you can breathe light and love into this darkness, and the world will reawaken. You create the night, and you create the dawn. This dawning is the first dawning. This first dawning is the glory of the world around you and the glory of your soul manifest in the world around you.

We say this again because we are the fourth gate. We ask you to maintain play in your passage through creation. We ask you not to hesitate to go forward with strength, with determination. Your guide does not hesitate, rather is full of life and hardiness. Be this way yourself.

Understand that you cannot withdraw from your own experience; you cannot withdraw from the experience of self. Realize, too, that you cannot take a respite from your world or from yourself, because a respite from yourself is one you can never take.

When you are feeling weary, take our hand. Do not attempt to retreat. You may feel lost, for we are moving forward. You may have to call out to us at the top of your lungs. Or, you may even have to find your own way, for a time. It is possible to do this. Be aware, however, that you can never rest. There is no respite from your true self. Instead, there is only inward motion. As you continue to evolve and grow, you leave those idiosyncrasies of self behind. The most important thing you take with you is your own flow of energy. In the same way as the heart pumps and lungs breathe, you take with you the flow of great energy. This is the most important truth which can be said about you. Know that energy is what guides you. You are in the flow and in the midst of things. Be one with this.

We wish you love from our heart. Know that we have spoken from our great strength to yours.

The Weaver

The Fifth Gate

Welcome to the fifth gate. I greet you from my place of work. I am the weaver. I am the master of that craft you see so beautifully carried out in those tropical regions of the world. We sit outside our homes under the sun, and upon our looms we create wonderful patterns of bright colors. Fields of cloth unfold from our looms. We seem to be content in what we do. If you watch us, sometimes the thought may cross your minds that we are plain, peasant people, content to do the simplest things in life. But, this would not be discernment on your part. We weave complex patterns. We enjoy the complexity of these systems which we have created. We feel that we know when to terminate what we have done and when to begin another pattern. My friends, upon your approach to the fifth gate, you must know that all your acts in this world have woven themselves into a pattern. This pattern is for you to see. And, upon seeing it, it is for you to know when it is fully realized and to execute its end.

Day after day, thought upon thought, act upon act, you weave patterns. These may seem coarse. They may seem to have great beauty. They may seem to be random. You have seen seemingly random patterns of cloth, have you not? You have also seen geometric designs, mathematically disciplined and perfect patterns. You have seen patterns into which are injected boldly contrasting colors and shapes.

In every case you must realize that within your life there comes a time for all patterns to be cut. And, you must realize that all patterns will be terminated. Nothing you can create, even those things you have created in the cumulative, cannot be ended by you. For we only have one loom on which we are working. We cannot weave two patterns at the same time. We must relieve the loom of the cloth which it made, or else that cloth can never be put to use. We must set upon the loom the new patterns for experience which derive from our hearts. It is our hearts, too, which tell us when to remove those patterns from our loom. It is your hearts which tell you when to remove those patterns of experience from your lives.

Weaving or cutting, picking up thread, you notice that we are content. This is not an arduous task. There is serenity and joy in what we do. There is beauty and grace in the movement of our hands. And there is wonder and mystery as the pattern unfolds. There is wonder at the dissolution of mystery as the pattern reveals itself. This is no burdensome labor. We do not sweat under the hot sun. Our backs are not hunched over. Our hands are not pricked and bleeding. We do not labor in great poverty. But, rather, we do what we do out of joy and a sense of fulfillment and a peace with the ending of all things.

You do not need to force yourself to discard your old self, your old patterns. You need to see them as they have unfolded. You need to see them in their fulfillment. And, you need to realize that whatever is fulfilled need not be worked on any longer. You can then cut away with joy those threads that bind the cloth to the loom.

In the programming that passes for education in your world, you have been taught that you are a product of your environment or of your genetics, that you have been conditioned to do this or conditioned to do that. You seek help in changing those patterns inside you. And yet, you do not think about the cloth itself. Some of you may understand us when we say, "Think of yourself as becoming a new being." Are there not times when you have met friends whom you have not seen in many long years, and some of them are yet laboring on the same cloth? Yet, there are others whom you meet who have gone through great transformations. They seem to be new people. It is possible for you to become reborn into the body with a greater sense of purpose and a refreshing new idea in your mind about who you are and what you can do.

If what I do is so simple, why is it so hard for you to know when it is time to cut? Why is it that you fumble and falter when it is time to pick up a new thread, or choose a color? You worry about the quality of your decisions and what is going happen to you, and so you stop.

It is impossible to know the future until you begin to weave it yourself. It is impossible to discern the quality of this fabric until the pattern is made clear by repetition. It is only through the senses of the heart that you know which instrument to place in your hand, and what color thread belongs in your fabric. You cannot rationalize what is yet unseen by you. Experience, like one cloth upon the other, gives you some confidence—as in leading many lives, you have confidence in this one. But, it does not create a guarantee. You must have the courage of heart to know how to begin again as well as how to end. If you are too dazzled by the brightness of the red and yellow colored thread you use, perhaps it is time for you to create a new cloth. If you feel it is time for you to find equanimity, maybe you could choose blues and purples, more subdued colors.

But choose you must, or else someone will choose these patterns for you. It is possible to fulfill a false prophecy as well as a true one. In creating cloth, it is possible for you to fulfill the wishes of others in creating cloth, rather than your own. If now in your life, you feel as if the sun is beating intensely upon your brow, if your back is hunched over, if your fingers are bleeding and sore, if you believe your work to be arduous and painful, you could be weaving a cloth that is not of your own choosing. We say: cut this cloth now. Engage in the joy, the lightness, and the beauty of creating from your own heart, knowing when to cut and when to commence creation anew. We represent the fifth gate. We represent it in love. But we must now go back to our work.

The next gate is no gate at all and is all gates at once. The next entity is All Entities.

The Sixth Gate

My children, I stand at the entrance to the sixth gate, that Being whom you call the Creator God. We are here only because there can be no other to show you this gate. This infinite gate is the last barrier you will cross into the level of soul which is the highest expression of self. For all this time you have been making and remaking yourself. All this time, throughout this book, you have been laboring at self, until self has become something that you think you can admire and love. Now, at this gate, we say to you that what must be discarded is not self, for this is a game. You cannot discard that which is the identity of your own thought. In the sixth gate you are rather asked to reconcile a duality that expresses itself in the words "doer" and "receiver."

Who is acting? Who is acted upon? In this gate you will know that there is no difference between who is acting and who is acted upon. In this gate you will know that there is no difference between who you are and who anyone else is. There is no barrier between yourself and the self of others. There is no demarcation line. When you cross the sixth gate, you see the world open before you, free of these thoughts which chain you, free of ego. The way through this gate is the way of love. Each footstep brings you closer to the Godhead, for I stand at this gate. I am This Gate. Consciousness of the Godhead is consciousness of this. We are All Things and we are No One Thing. You have tried to put labels on God, and there are no labels that are suitable. You have said that God is This and God is That, God is Love and God is Wrath, God is The World and God is Beyond The World. All these words fall down feebly in their inadequacy, ineffective. I am All Things. I am No One Thing. To partake of the Godhead is to know that you, also, are no one thing at any time or at any place, and to know that you are all things. These steps that you take in love bring you to a feeling which is beyond feeling, which is knowledge beyond knowledge. It is a realm of infinite knowing and infinite compassion. There, at last self can be at peace. There, at last the mind has found a place to rest from its meanderings. This is not the death of anything; it is the rebirth of the soul in the body.

Who does and who does not? You are My children. It is of no importance to Me who acts and who is acted upon, what you believe you are doing, and what you believe others are doing. I must address you all, universally, as individuals. I speak to each one of you, and yet I address all of you at once every time I do speak.

Thus, you must proceed onward through this gate of the endless embracing of the world in compassion. You have faltered, fallen short at times, not realizing that I have allowed you to experience on your earthly plane for the purpose of educating you in this respect. And you do not know that in passing judgment on your own soul, you, in turn, attribute judgment to Me. It is burdensome to take on judgment, and I will not do it. The opposite drive from compassion is that of judgment. It is that of deciding who has done right and who has done wrong. But it is beyond this. It is deciding who has done and who has not done. This also is a great trap and a great pain from which you need to be delivered. It is not important anymore in this sixth gate who has done. It is only important that you love.

God's judgment does not exist. I sit in judgment of no one. When the most atrocious act you can imagine manifests itself, I have nothing but love for the being who perpetrated it. When the most horrific acts take place in the world, I embrace those acts themselves in My love, My compassion. Who, as God, would not have compassion for what they see? When the true self gets lost and the desire to do unloving things becomes realized in someone, you must know that I have nothing but love for that lost soul.

The only response you must have to others has always been and will always be love. The only true choice you have is what form love will take. This sixth gate is that of great compassion. It is compassion for all beings, compassion for each being as if they were all beings. And, this compassion, my children, begins with your own decree of self-acceptance. For who in this world has not been subject to pain and vicissitudes? Who has not done things which they later regret?

My children, you must understand that as I am here in this realm of yours not to judge but to love, this infinite compassion must begin with yourself, for you are that which keeps Me alive. By holding Me inside you, you keep Me alive in this realm. So, the greatest compassion is that which you must have for self.

I have felt anger and denial coming from many souls in this world. When you begin to judge events, you judge God. When you begin to have compassion for what has occurred, not just for the souls around you, you begin to have compassion for God, and you begin to drop your judgment of God. Likewise, this compassion for God enables you to have compassion for the God inside you, for that spark of Divinity inside you, for that burning light above the heart which is your soul.

Compassion is infinite in its own nature and must be put in terms of infinity to make sense. Compassion is, by its very nature, infinite and mighty. From this point of self love in your own soul, you reach out to all creation in compassion. You show love and compassion to each and every thing and all those things that are not things, that have no thingness.

We are Love because it is Our nature to love. We are Great because it is Our nature. We are Infinite—We can stretch out Our Hands into the immense universe. And all My properties of self are encapsulated in that which you call the Light of your soul. When this Light burns brightest, it burns with the fire of compassion and love.

Eventually, my children, you will get to the sixth gate. You may have not wanted to approach it, but it is there for you. Eventually, this sixth gate speaks out and tells you of your own God-nature. It seems to be a responsibility you cannot handle, but that is an illusion. Compassion is not a responsibility; it is a state of being. So, there is no longer that pause of silence between thought and action.

There is no response now that is needed. You are, simply, in a state of great compassion, not caring who is doing and who is being acted upon, not caring if you are the doer or receiver. You look through the window of the soul into the great beauty of this world, and you no longer care who is looking through the window. You engage in acts of love without thought as to whether there is an individual center to that activity which can be called your self.

The freedom that this existence gives you is great. You no longer fear God, because you no longer feel the need to separate yourself from God. You no longer fear self. You no longer tremble with fearful thoughts of karma and destiny, of prefigurements of the future. You no longer fear the painful memories of the past. You sit knowing that there is no one who is sitting. You sit in your self knowing that there is no self. The realm of compassion, the sixth gate, is one of great breadth and beauty. It is one of infinite love. Begin this gate by loving what is nearest to you. End it by loving what is unseen by you.

My children, I will not stay longer. It is not MY intention to give you words and not allow you time to realize those words. Know that nothing you do is drifting away from Me. As you have touched the pages of this book, as you have listened to the written word, you cannot be far from Me. You cannot be without my embrace. My love is not stretching out from the vastness of space to you. For you are the one before Me. You are the one who is before me whom I choose to love.

PART TWO

Healing

Preface

We again bring you greetings from the Source of All Light and Love. This is Lenonda.

It is not important that you fully realize the steps in the prior section of the Path. It is only important that, in some way, you have internalized them. It is impossible to fully realize yourself as a Creator God in one life. In many, many lifetimes you are required to relive your essence as Creator Gods, until you own what you are and fully put into practice and fully live out your essence. It is, likewise, impossible for us to say to you that you must be on the highest planes of compassion before you move onward. It is impossible for us to say to you that you must be in the highest state of consciousness, likewise, to receive the blessings of the God Light. It is impossible for us to say to you that you are in need of perfection, because we would not be able to place that demand upon you, unless we ourselves are in a perfect state.

We have served also in this place where you live. Though you have simply received the mere promise of compassion from the Path, you must now believe that you can live it out as beings of Light and Love. In this belief, you are required to do certain things. Yet this belief does not subjugate you, but motivates you. It does not draw its own consequences, but it tells you to do things in love.

In compassion you are required to move into healing. Love places a demand upon you. It is an impetus to heal. It is quite natural and profound. It is a journey into the Christ Light, and it is a journey into the full realization of the potential for love. And this is the beginning of Book 2, Part 2 of the Path. The Path is, as you will see later on in the book, not set. It is not rigid. We simply stop at Part 5 and do not go forward, because, otherwise, we would be endlessly speaking of the Path. At a certain point you must come to a realization which is one of great profundity, but not a realization we can grant you. It is only something we can share with you. It will come at the very end.

Now, we ask you once again to make sure that, when you are reading, you are in the quietness of your day—the most silent and peaceful part. We ask you to center yourself in love, because to hear without love is a great burden, and it causes great deception. If you listen in love, you are better able to enjoy the Path and to reach the fulmination of love. If you listen without love, then mind is loosened to roam without direction, without guidance, and without a center. The mind does not center itself. It is the heart which centers the mind. So, remember, your acceptance or rejection of this book is im-material to us. And, likewise, your rejection or acceptance of one or more parts of it is immaterial to us. Simply put aside what does not ring true for you. Remember that we have channeled one entity after another in each chapter and will continue this process until you real-ize what is going on.

In the world you are most blessed with friends and lovers, of all races, species and all natures. Enjoy what is given to you by God, right now. Enjoy this message from the Source. It is one which also informs you of your own lineage and your own contact in love. As you feel intimacy and mutual love coming from each and every being channeled, it is most important that you realize your ease with them is also a recognition of the Divine Nature you share. If you cannot share in Divine Love, then you need to stop reading entirely. But, we believe for most of you, love is so well established within that you will resonate with what is being told to you.

You must read in realization and allow yourself to move through this part of the dance. And the dance in these next four sec-tions is becoming more and more your own, until Part 5 when you will see the realization of your own dance. But you must go through movements of the dance with some kind of respect for sequence. Al-though linear time does not govern the dance, a sequence of move-ments determines that there is a dance. And this is what we would like to share with you right now. In Part 2, the dance is to the Christ Light and to healing.

In this sense you are at one with what is going on, because you realize that no part of the dance can be extracted and yet have meaning. The segments of dance have meaning in context alone. By themselves, they fall down, and no matter how beautiful and loving they seem of themselves, they cannot complete the dance. That the dance, ultimately, must be completed by you is the wisdom of the Path. But even these parts we give you cannot be understood by examining their individual segments of movement, and individual gestures.

So, it is with great love and joy that we leave now to share with you on another level at some later time. We will introduce all parts. Part 2, as we said, is one of movement toward the Christ Light and, therefore, toward healing. You may believe that nothing could happen afterward, but if that were true, all life would have ceased when the Christ Light came. And that is not what the Christ Light brings.

So, good-bye and God bless you in your journey to God.

The Angel of Death

⊙ The First Gate

We bring you greetings in love and joy, for I speak to you in joy, and I would not speak beyond the connection to you in joy. When the centers of compassion are stirred, and your contact with God is compassionate, it is love which comes to you. You are compelled to go forward, compelled in the most meaningful way possible, in the way of love. The way of love is like a vibration within you that is, at the same time, a calling. And the calling is a most alluring one, yet it is a calling to the path of healing. You need to understand that you cannot escape what is before you in this path, that all love impels you to heal. It impels you to heal that which is yet unhealed. It is calling you. The world of compassion for all beings calls upon you to bring forth healing from your essence. If love is the basis of your soul, then you must know that healing accompanies it.

If it can be said that the universe was created directly out of God, it was created out of a paradox. The paradox of creation became the paradox of the One and the many. It is not our place, now, to interpret this paradox, but to offer you a parallel one. The paradox is that, when the Light of God's compassion courses through you, you feel at the same time the need to heal. It is not the objectivity of science, nor the coldness of observation, nor the fear of death which draws up the realization of the need to heal something. It is God's infinite compassion that in a great paradox calls upon you to recognize the need for healing. Without the compassion which is love, there is no true recognition of the need for healing; there is no true desire for healing; there is no true impetus to heal. Without love, there is no direction to healing; there is no essence in healing. Couched in scientific terms and pushed forward by the intellect, healing becomes dark, vacuous and impotent. When you see true healing in the world around you, you see healing that is ultimately guided, motivated, and supported by love. Healing described through science, technology, professionalism, rationalism, institutionalism, or anything less than God-driven compassion is false healing. Anything that does heal is healed only through compassion. Compassion irrevocably calls forth healing.

It is a paradox to be in compassion and at once to see that there is need of healing. It is as if the One and the many have shown themselves to each other. And it is as if you are compelled, therefore, to bring resolution to them. What is to be healed has fragmented itself from the One. It needs to reconcile itself to the One, but not to disappear, because to disappear would mean that there would be no tension left, and the loss of its identity would make the paradox a false one, which it is not.

Infinite compassion calls forth constant healing, and who could be so perfect that they do not need healing? Who is so one with the Infinite God that they have no need to ask for healing? Any time, my friends, that you have a place in which more Light can come, in which more dark can be released, there is a place where you need healing. In each of us, we see to a greater or lesser degree the need to heal something. And, we say to ourselves that it is impossible for us to be of the Light and need healing at the same time. But this is a confusion of the mind which often tells us that we are not good enough to be in the Light. Being of God, in the state of infinite compassion, is seeing that there is healing needing to be done within us. It is, in fact, in the state of oneness with God in compassion that we see there is an abundant need to heal.

We are called forth to do the healing both on ourselves and on others. If we and all others are part of the same manifestation, if we cannot truly draw the line between who is doing and who is receiving, then we must say that if one needs healing, then all need healing. Or, if we live in infinite compassion, we cannot separate ourselves, therefore, from anyone else and say that our own healing is complete, but another is in need of healing. For there can be no intrinsic difference between the One and the many. There cannot be any difference between who does and who receives; who has done and who has not done. Therefore, you cannot say, "Healing is necessary for this one or for that one, but not for me."

So, I come to you as an angel, which is what I am in your terminology, and I speak to you as one who brings about healing. I come to you as one who speaks to you of healing for yourself. For, as we say, it is the most logical, the most correct, and the most loving place to begin healing. And, it is the place to begin healing in which there is the least amount of denial. For, as much as you may hide darkness from yourself, the admission to yourself that you are in need of some healing, however incomplete that admission, is always greater than the acknowledgment of another's need of healing, since you cannot heal another as well as you can yourself. And in the admission that you are in need of healing, you are truthfully acknowledging your lack of separation from God and from God's Creation in which you have manifested self, and of which you are a distinct part at the same time. Because the Source of all Light is God, the Source of all healing Light is God. To recognize the need for healing inside you, is to be willing to draw in Light, profound and beautiful Light, but Light directed toward healing in love.

At this time we do not want to describe to you God's Light, because that will be part of the process later on, and we do not wish to usurp another's position by speaking to you of the Light itself. We come to you to allow the process of acknowledgment of the need to heal to take place. Being of the angelic realm, it is my responsibility, and my joy and pleasure, as strange as this may seem to you, to be a messenger for you of the need to heal. It is, in fact, that I am the messenger of your death and of the death of many others. It is beings, such as myself, of the angelic realm who announce your death, who are messengers of that final release and final healing, that you receive in body, which is a release from the body itself. It is this call to you, not that something is wrong or that you have reached the end of your life, but that you have spoken out in some inner place in your soul and have asked for release from this lifetime. I feed this realization back to you. I deliver to you the thought that death is release, and not the end of existence. But, of course, in knowing this, you still recoil from me, because you believe I hold terrible things within my robes— disease, violence, or hatred of God. But this is not the case. It is rather that, as I come to you, I show to you that this journey of your soul is nearing its completion. It is possible that disease or violent death may come to you. It is also possible that those who hold hatred in their heart for God may rob you of your body's vitality. But it is also your soul which has called out for healing. And this is not a message which is easy for anyone to receive.

I knock on your door. I introduce myself. You are slow to let me in, but my message is so loud and firm that you cannot avoid confronting me. Your soul has spoken out and has asked for release from whatever negativity it has. It could be that, in the manner of the tiger, a violent act will remove the soul from the body, which is in such need of healing that your soul cries out for some great drama to take place. It could be that disease comes to you, and this disease is summoning healing power to you. And it could be you see that this Light of healing has been enough, that the body, as an experiment of soul, has lost its usefulness to you.

It is not that I bring disease to you, my friends, or violence. It is that I make you aware of an impassioned plea of the soul for release. Enough healing has been done for you in this lifetime, and you need to go on to other lives. Enough healing work has been done by you, and this final healing is in need of taking place. It may not seem complete. If it were, it could mean the true death of the soul. It is not complete death for the soul, but it is death expressing in body.

With all healing, as with all disease, each separate act of healing is like a death for the body. The body must die to that which needs to be released, and to be reborn. Who wants to have a cancerous growth inside them, festering and growing to infinity? You would seek to be released from that diseased tissue. But likewise, you would seek the death of disability, of absence, of problems arising in the system, and of emotions which cannot find resolution. You ask for release from all forms of darkness inside you, one by one perhaps, but for all of them.

The announcement that something must die to you is my service. The announcement of your death is also that of your disease, of your body in crisis, or the crises of the mind and of the heart. It is the message that healing is in need of taking place. This is a beautiful time in which you know there must be God. For love commands healing. Therefore, behind each command for healing you must know that there is a God of infinite compassion and that you can partake of this God nature by healing. The first healing which comes to you is that of healing self. It is the first of which you must be aware. You cannot separate yourself from others, and yet in this long lifetime, you have a starting point, and this is yourself.

Sometimes the healing messages the angels give are messages sent by others. Because you have a genuine need to heal yourself, you feel a desire to heal others. The spurning of others because of their need to heal is, in the same manner, a rejection of God's healing Light for your self. Although no one's healing is perfectly the same as another's, when you see others in their need to heal and repel them in judgment, you likewise repel healing for yourself. The acceptance in love that you, as well as everyone, are in need of healing is an acceptance of your own compassionate nature derived from God, and an acceptance of your own healing.

When you recognize that there is a self in need of healing, the ego arises to claim self. And when the ego does so, all thoughts of healing begin to become tainted. Even after I have left my message, you are wrestling with ego in an attempt to reconcile yourself to healing. It is a process that you must go through. It becomes easier and easier as you journey through life, but it is a process, nevertheless, of letting go of ego and of self. The self will die as you heal, and the ego is what holds the reins of self and which does not want to let go.

To drop the illusion of separateness, one also needs to embrace the idea of connectiveness, even connection to darkness. So, it is frightening for the soul to so look upon itself in darkness and in ego. However, the ego holds the reins of self, and self wants to say, "I am not touched by darkness. This darkness is not me." It is true that it is not you. Darkness is not self. But self is not God or soul. Ego wants to say, "I am not this darkness, so it cannot touch me." Or, it wants to say, "Since darkness has touched me, I am mired in self, because self, having darkness in it, is separate from God. God is Light and not darkness. So, this healing cannot take place, because self alone cannot heal self, cannot destroy its own identity." This is ego speaking. You are not separate from God. Remember also that you have tiger energy in you, and remember that self can destroy self. It may embrace another illusion of self, but so be it. We plunge into healing, and we take that chance. We say that it is better to make the attempt than not. It is better to work in the Light imperfectly than to allow ego to direct us and to drive us into darkness. For who is not touched by darkness? It was God, in the dawn of creation, sensing darkness around Her, who summoned forth all of creation. You are here because even God, in a sense, understood the need for healing self.

So, to push this darkness away from you is not ungodly. It is this need to fix yourself in a certain spot that is centered in self or ego and not in love, which causes disease to come to you. To the extent some part of you is yet centered in self, you have drawn darkness to you. And the need to heal is also the need to move forward into the fullness of your God-nature, the nature of an Infinitely Compassionate and an Eternally Creating God.

We bring you the call for the need to release. You must recognize the need to heal. Understand it is not a call saying that you are lacking in love, or that you are not the Creator God you believe you are, or that God's nature is not your nature. You are indivisible from God nature. It is the case, in fact, that the call to heal is the call back to the fullness of your God nature and a call away from the darkness. In recognizing that you need to heal, without having to see anyone else as needing healing, you accept the call to release yourself from all that is unloving and to embrace everything that comes to you as part of this Infinitely Compassionate God.

Do you imagine that healing takes place so that you could become the healer? You would be a fool to think this, and you now are beyond this fool barking a dialogue with self. It is compassion that first calls forth the need for healing. But, it is not until you have love in your heart, and so are able to witness God's infinite compassion, that you actually realize the need for healing. It is only then, in love, do you will yourself to heal.

So rejoice, my friends, that you have discovered something which needs release in you. Rejoice in this path of healing, the path of your wholeness and your oneness.

God bless you, and I bid you good-bye.

◭ The Second Gate

W e bring joy and greetings from the Godhead. We are here with you as you read. Your blessed purpose on this Earth has never been to do something for others—it has been for you to create. But, we believe that to speak of creation without healing is a great injustice. It is not possible to create where another already has created. But, to know where you or another has created is not as important as to see creation constantly unfolding. Yet, there is also a great need to see before you where things are still in darkness, where nothing emerges that can truly be called creation.

What lies in darkness calls forth your creative power to heal. It is your power, but it is God who feeds you this energy of creation. And healing is a form of creation—in fact, the most fundamental form of creation there is. Creation allows you to see the difference between what is in the Light and what is in the darkness. For you would not want to see this if you did not have that creative power to heal within you. It would be a terrible crime for God to send you the angel of death and let you hear its wisdom without enabling you to have the means to heal. It is, therefore, the benevolence of God, the Loving God, which allows you to partake of God's own nature. It is, therefore, the acceptance of God's nature, the nature of healing creation which first enables you to accept there is something in need of healing. Without this empowerment, you would never come to a place of understanding, love, and compassion. And, is that not how you got to your own empowerment as a compassionate being, by feeling the energy to act in the world first, and then realizing that the Source of this energy was God? You were as abundantly full of this energy as you wished to be; you became creative and compassionate, and you are healing. It would be bitter irony for you to watch yourself in a world in need of healing and to think that nothing you can do could heal.

At this point, a thought might be coming to you that you have witnessed people with illnesses for which there are no cures. Then you say to us, "If there is infinite healing power coming from God and you can draw upon this power, and if the Infinitely Loving God has endowed you with infinitely loving and creative qualities, how is it possible, therefore, that someone has illness for which there is no apparent cure?" And I ask you, if this is the case, to find your calm center again—that of love—and accept that you do not always know what is being healed or how it is being healed. It is easy for you to say, "I have, in clinging to self, taken in the wrong food." Or, "I need healing of heart, because I have embraced the wrong lover out of darkness." Or, "I have gotten myself in, and I must get myself out." Those, in a way, can be very liberating thoughts. But, then, you see yourself in trauma and say, "Could I have engendered such violence to myself?" Or, you see yourself in a diseased state and find that you must live in this state for the remainder of your life. You then say to yourself, "How am I to heal? If this power is mine, then I must be able to heal everything. This power must enable me to heal all the dark-ness in me, and, therefore, I will be free of this malady which plagues my system. If I have drawn this crisis of the physical or emotional body to me, I must be able to draw in equal amounts of healing."

We know that in our lives this could not be entirely true. What often happens to you is that the self decides it is the arbiter of what is healing and what is not. Who knows what is being healed— what is coming from the darkness and what is coming from the Light? If you are asked to heal all aspects of self, then one aspect of self must balance itself out against the other. And you must see that you are more than one mere physical or emotional being, that you are a spiri-tual one, too. This other form of self which is spirit is also in need of healing and also must play out its healing through the emotional self or through the body self, and you must see that you are not to judge in what form the healing takes place. It could be that those paralyzed bring great healing to themselves. You must be aware that those in the wheelchair do not have darkness in them for that. They may, in fact, be healing an unseen disease. The healing may take on higher aspects through that body.

So, you are to proceed forward without judgment, for judgment will stop you from attaining healing. When you have healed as a whole being, you will know where one aspect of self has played against the other, and you will know what the purpose in your disease has been. But, until then, you must accept that God's way is a loving way. And although you may have called upon yourself all illness and trauma, all pain on the physical or the emotional level, yet you may not know what truly needs to be healed. You must be without judgment for yourself. Once you hear the call of the angel of death, you must accept that you cannot whittle down your perception into such specifics that you are able to understand the nature of the healing, until you have completed it.

So now, your ability to accept God's loving energy may be hampered by your clinging to judgment. Be mindful that this could be the second gate for you to cross: to free yourself from the bonds of judgment once again. As you have freed your mind, you need to free your heart and body from judgments. Then, the ability to receive God's abundant energy will come forth in you. You will receive it, or you will not heal. You can receive it because you are the Creator God. The fact that you are this being of infinite compassion enables you to receive it. Let it pour forth to you.

I am a deva of the forest, and I work with the water energy. You travel far in this world, and in your travels you always seek to rest at the spot where water flows from the Earth. You get nourishment and you get healing from the water which flows out of fountains and brooks and the streams and lakes of the Earth. We ourselves roll in this fresh water, and we take in the luxury of the healing properties it gives us. We bring forth water energy from the center of the Earth. Even that distance is not too far. This force of healing is ours. If you travel through the woods and you stumble and fall, saying to yourself that life is painful, that you must face sickness, that you are this being whose life is suffering, then you will never find yourself in the place where you can be refreshed, where the water flows over the rocks - clear, cool, and nourishing.

So, we are here to help in the Second Gate of healing, to help you know that Light pushes away darkness, and that all of your life need not be suffering. There are moments of joy and healing in it, if you are willing to accept.

My friends, we go, and God bless you.

The Third Gate

I bring you greetings. I am the angel of birth. We are here in order to talk to you about the form in which healing takes place. You have been told the awareness that healing is needed is not of darkness. It is of the Light, and it propels you toward healing. We have also told you God's energy is the source of all healing, is abundant, and is there for you to take. You need not struggle for it—and this is the second realization you must have. Now, this next part, with which you must come to terms, is the form in which healing comes.

If God's healing energy is as flowing water, then from what vessel is this water drunk? Form has been a very great problem for many of the souls on the planet. You must know that the form which something takes is of God in the same way that what pours itself into form is of God. Who does the healing and who receives the healing is at issue, because form also involves what is healed and what does the healing. After all, we know that God's energy is the true source of any healing. But we also know, being creatures of the practical world, that this healing energy must be embodied in some form.

We offer you a warning to avoid those who assume that they heal without acknowledging God's healing Light. Ultimately, they will not be able to heal you. It is, in fact, only those who acknowledge the energy coming from God that can be your greatest healers. This, however, does not answer the question, "Who does the healing, and who receives the healing?" You have been told before who has done and who has not done is illusory. Yet, here in this path to healing you seek out a healer, so you ask yourself what if anything to invest in duality.

Let us examine the role of the healer. It is as necessary to examine this as to understand that there is someone to be healed. If you were to study healing of some kind, whether it be that of the spirit, the emotions or the body, eventually, you come to the point where you turn inward and ask yourself if you are truly to be healed, and who is to heal you. At some point, you should see yourself, not as someone who takes on the illness of others or has a heightened awareness of illness as you are treating others, but as someone who comes to a heightened consciousness that you yourself are in need of healing and that your first and best use of your healing skills is to heal yourself. There is no one in the world who has not crossed this bridge and can call themselves a true healer. And it does not serve to think that someone could heal all aspects of self equally by themselves, but it is the way of God that one thing of self, at least, is given to each healer to heal themselves.

Indeed, healers set out to heal a part of themselves, whether it is working through an emotional or a physical ailment. In coming to terms with their own intrinsic need to heal, they come to acceptance of self and, therefore, acceptance of their clients, even though their clients are not yet healed. And, in healing themselves, they come to know the nature of healing, being both the giver and the receiver of the healing embodied.

But they also come to terms with release and judgment. It is easy to believe that you work with miracles, when you are working with such seemingly new and powerful techniques of healing—it is a very great temptation. You would not want to say that you would forego any new developments in your profession, but there is also a tendency to believe that the newest ones empower you to be God. This judgment of the healer means that the healer ultimately must admit that they are not God. Although they have use of God's power, they cannot be The One God. This comes to all in some life, in some form, when someone has made the soul decision to be a healer.

It is likewise so, that those who seek healing present themselves as a reflection of the healer. And if judgment has been released, the healer can see with empathy and compassion the soul which is in need of healing. Or, they can look with derision and judgment upon that person, if they have not yet crossed this threshold.

In the eyes of the one to be healed, there is also a transition to be made. The healer at first becomes all powerful. All trust and faith is given to the healer. Then, at some point, there is some realization that the one who receives the healing must be their own healer. For the healer designated by the one who is to be healed cannot sustain this healing energy throughout the days and the nights in which healing takes place. The one who ostensibly performs the healing is the one who is most directing the energy at a given moment, but it is the person who is to be healed who must maintain this energy with them at all times, and to receive this energy in even greater quantity than the healer has directed.

The energy whose Source is God cannot discriminate between who has been assigned the task of healing and who has been assigned the task of receiving the healing. It does not know direction until it strikes the self and that self determines how the energy is going to be used. All loving energy from God is personal. That is to say, it is the peculiarity of healing that it can be received personally, even if it appears to come from the most impersonal Source in the universe, the impersonal aspects of God. But when striking the self, it gathers momentum and force at the same time. And then, how it becomes directed is determined by what the thought of self is. If someone is determined to be the healer, then that force of energy bypasses them and goes directly into the being who is to be healed. Inevitably, this method hurts the healers, because they were not willing to receive the energy which they transmit, and the healers become corrupt, unable to do healing. So, if your notions of self say that you cannot heal another without first healing yourself, that you cannot be the healer without being the healed, then you will be able to go forward and transmit great energy. To the extent that the self is healed in this matter and this dualism has been revoked, the healer is entitled to get enormous energy through them, because they are willing in body to be the vessel of that energy in total part.

Dualities such as these are not resolved by working with another. As soon as you identify someone as other than you, you have created a duality, and since no dualities are dissimilar or disconnected from each other, you cannot work through this duality and discover who or what really is healed and who or what really is not. So, duality is always torn apart from the inside without regard to what, if anything, is beyond self.

Duality is always destroyed from within. It is the acceptance that you are the healer and the healed at the same time which destroys the duality. And it is likewise so for those receiving healing energies. They will receive it through the healer in great abundance only if they allow themselves to let this energy empower them, to affect and to bring to a close the healing themselves, because no healing is complete without the healed seeing themselves also as the healer.

It is possible for you to be healed by a less-than-perfect individual, is it not? It is, in fact, impossible to be healed by anyone but an imperfect being, since there is nothing before you in the world that is perfect. It is possible that you, as the healer of self, are able to heal in a state of imperfection. For you are not God, either. God's energy will strike you and illuminate self first, in order to show you what you think of self, and how self is working with you or against you. There is no healing in which self is not confronted and destroyed. If there is healing to be done, self must be dismembered. The healer, in whatever practice they have, must let go of the reins of self and give up the desire to perpetuate self, and must give themselves to the moment and see that response in love is more important than clinging to self through ego. And, those healed after searching extensively for the right healer, and studying at length, must give up notions of self. It is not only because these notions have drawn darkness to them, but also because it is impossible to receive true healing in the limited form which any one self could swallow. In the transition between one self dying and a new self emerging, but not the obliteration of self, all of God's infinite energy can come through. In the surrender of self, you allow a healed self to emerge.

God, in Her infinite wisdom, has appointed a great many healers in the universe. It can be said that everyone engaged in God's business is a healer. But every appointment is not always an appointment from God. Be aware that those who offer themselves as healers have need to prove to you their lineage; they need to show you their direct connection to God. This will be manifest in some form, if you ask for it. Words spoken are cheap, and something of darkness can parrot to you the proverbs of Light without much hesitation. But we want to say, be aware that everything which is truly of healing is a one-step connection to God. Lineage as a healer is the direct contact with God. And it needs to be shown and accepted before any healing properly takes place. Ask for it, and you will see some sign of it. Do not ask for it, and you beg trouble.

Is it possible for God to heal directly? We say there is a great blessing in the universe that this does occur. God heals directly in partnership with the healed. After all, you, in being healed are still the healer, and God in healing you is the Healing God. You are part of God. Your partnership with God can take many forms. Direct healing can be yours. Not everyone does experience it, but everyone can. And this great blessing is beyond words. We may be asking for your trust to say that healing does, in fact, take place directly from God. But, we do not believe it will strain credulity to say that all healing takes place in partnership. It is a partnership with one's self and a partnership with the external form of the healing and the soul of your healer.

In this gate, you ask for acceptance of the form in which healing comes. It is sometimes a form which you believe you could not have chosen in love. It is sometimes a form on which you can see the blemishes very lucidly. Can you be accepting of the healer? Can you be accepting of the person to be healed? You are one and the same, but, can you do it? The threshold is exactly this. We have said that no healer is perfect and that you must complete your own healing. Could it be that you go from healer to healer, until you find that you have enough of a picture to close the healing? This is possible. Is it possible you have such an acute problem that one healer will be able to enter the gate and help you? This is possible also. And from the aspect of a healer, is it possible for someone to come to you and for them to depart from you having been incomplete in their healing and to see another as the next step in their healing? This is quite possible. Is it possible that you work with them until they realize they need to heal themselves and then withdraw from you? This is possible also. Whatever it may be, acceptance is in order. The more you pin your hopes and expectations on a demigod, the more you will be disappointed. The more readily you are able to come to terms with your own dark places and the dark places of others, the better you are able to heal. Who is to do the healing for you if you do not first have acceptance of form? Ultimately, it could be that form replaces ideas of self, and that you accept form in its incompleteness or imperfection, and attain greater closeness to your God-nature through it.

We thank you. God bless you.

The Fourth Gate

This is the Archangel Ariel. I bring you greetings through God's
healing energy.

Let us say that you are struggling at this time with all of your
tactics for dealing with your darkness, or the darkness of others, and
you are attempting to make healing possible. You see your starting
point as being either the person healed or the person healing. You
wish to do the best, to command the greatest degree of healing energy, and you wish to dispel darkness. This darkness could take the
form of a cancerous growth, or a psychosis, or a chronic illness, or an
addiction, and you wish to bring it into the Light. You say to yourself,
"I see it in pain, and therefore I know it must also be displeasing to
God. I want to dispel this darkness and bring in Light in its place."
You have seen that the first two gates were those of seeing the darkness, wanting to dispel it, and wanting to bring in the God Light. It is
time for you now to release the tension in the process, in the same
way that you release the tension which held thoughts of self and inhibited healing energy to come through you. It takes time to heal,
and as you work through the process, you say, "How much do I wish
now to release, and how much Light do I need to bring in?"

Let us speak to you about the powers of the universe. If you
have an infestation of darkness from which you wish to be healed,
you inject God's Light into that spot, and, yet, if you are not ready to
release that dark and fetid part of you, you will not be healed. Likewise, if you pull the darkness out and you are not ready to fill that
empty part with Light, you will succumb to illness once again. There
is no force of God which does not have its complement. So, as God's

abundant Light comes through, the willingness to release calls forth another force. This is the energy of chaos and disintegration, of that which is not held by the will in Light and Love. The darkness within you needs to be broken, extracted and relinquished to God.

If God is yanking it back again, does God desire the darkness to be with Her? No, but God desires to cast this illusory matter into the void. This dark matter is corrupt and repugnant, and is what can be called negativity. God wishes to spread it in its appropriate place as a farmer would spread manure, and then to allow growth to come from it. But it cannot be that it is placed near living beings. God must pass it into the void in order for it to bring forth fruit. Since you are not this emptiness, allow God's disintegrating energy to release negativity from you, at the same time in which you are asking God Light to come to you.

Both energies need to be held in balance, and it is most important for you to perceive them in balance. If you believe in karmic debt, then you must separate yourself from your assets in order to make the payment; you must be willing to draw off part of your Light. But, if you have an enlightened view that you cannot have a true karmic debt, then it is doubly necessary for you to retain the Light in the knowledge that you can instead allow darkness to disintegrate and drift to God. Everything that you do in your imperfection has some darkness to it. No matter how greatly the body desires to be part of God, you have, in some way, darkness in every bit of Light. The angel of birth has explained to you that you are not perfect, but I am here to explain to you what to do with your imperfections.

What can you do with this darkness but offer it back to God? God knows what to do with darkness. This is how the universe became manifest. God drew Light out of darkness, splitting the darkness and creating the universe. You, as well, need to feel that you have this power to crack the darkness with Light, to dispel the darkness and direct it back to God—not out of hatred or out of judgment of God, but in the knowledge that God will do something with it which will, ultimately, be of the Light. You cannot proceed forward without this necessary balance between the darkness you remove and the Light you restore. When you are voiding darkness, you are no longer just the type of healer that you think you could have been. You are not directing Light then as much as calling directly upon God to extract darkness. You do not want to touch it. You do not want to pass the darkness through yourself the way you would want to pass Light through. You are, instead, asking God to use the gravity of the void to pull it out.

My friends, be careful what darkness you handle. You cannot heal darkness. It is not your place to put Light on darkness. You are not going to heal yourself or another by trying to heal their darkness. You cannot do it. Darkness is darkness and cannot be healed. When Light splits the darkness asunder, it is Light and it is no longer darkness. You cannot move darkness into Light, or else it would not be darkness. You can only split it apart. Let God initiate this splitting. It is God alone who can. Let God allow the darkness to gravitate to Her manure pile. God pulls the darkness toward Her and then allows it to be diverted into the pit of darkness. You must not handle it.

I, myself, the Archangel Ariel will not touch darkness. I will not handle it. I use my instruments and will not touch darkness. I will greet any soul in love and Light, and I will touch them with my loving hands, but I will not handle their darkness. If you find that you are trying to engage darkness in your life in an attempt to heal yourself or another, please refrain, for you are attempting something impossible. Think about the consequences. If you go to someone and say, "I want to heal your illness, so, I give it love and Light," you will be absorbed by that darkness. You can only heal the body, soul, spirit, and emotions of an individual. You cannot heal their disease. You cannot heal their addictions. The more Light you give darkness, the more darkness absorbs the Light. You need instead to ask God to pull this darkness out. You can wrap it in Light, as one would wrap a blanket around something which they did not want to touch. But you cannot give it Light. It will take your Light and make more darkness out of it. You can crack it with Light and split it apart into fragments and then have God take those fragments away, but darkness is not what you are attempting to heal.

Remember that by investing in self you may also invest in your self the ability to heal disease. Every time society believes it has healed a disease, Light takes that disease and changes the form of it, so that people see that darkness cannot be healed, that they must confront the soul of the individual and bring healing to the person and not to the disease. Did you eliminate diseases from the world when you found your cures? All cures have in them, now, the potential for more illness. No matter how diligently you are working to cure a disease, if you are working only to cure the disease and not working to bring love, healing and health to the individual, then you will find yourself in a fool's game. All healing is to be done on living beings of Light. You simply cannot heal disease; you will only proliferate disease in your attempt. You will allow its forms to multiply. And, at some point, those working only for the healing of the body may realize that their catalog of diseases is growing. What they are doing in actuality is increasing the number of diseases in the world by trying to put Light on darkness, by trying to heal disease, instead of delivering healing to the individual soul. When not bothering to heal the whole body systemically, they bring more disease as it alters itself.

God allows this to happen until love is called upon. Love needs to be manifest in the healing arts in a way which it has not existed, but which could be far in the future. Those who pursue healing in love from that place of infinite compassion know that Light cannot heal darkness and do not invest energy in duality. If there is darkness and Light, they already coexist. You do not need to take in darkness to have internal balance. You are Light, and darkness will always contrast itself against you. There is no need to internalize this duality.

When you see anything, you see Light. When you do not see anything, there is darkness and denial. Darkness brings you to denial, and, in denial, you will not believe that you have an illness, or that there is anything wrong. The recognition that healing needs to be taking place, ultimately will drive you to the affirmation of God's Light. One only discerns darkness by the Light around it. The overcoming of denial about the darkness yet within you is in reality a recognition of God's Light. So, in this way, bring yourself to healing by embracing the Light and letting it crack open the darkness. Do not feel that you must be in balance between Light and dark. The universe will find its balance without you internalizing duality.

As you go from one healing method to another in search of what will bring you almost to completeness, remember that in all these things, the overcoming of duality must take place. This true balance is not in shedding Light on darkness, but in releasing darkness, and, at the same time, quenching your thirst for Light. What you release and what you take in, what you give away and what you receive, is where your true balance is. Acknowledge this, enjoy it, and love it.

And go with God.

The Elephant

◉ The Fifth Gate

F rom all those precious places on Earth upon which our great feet tread, we bring you love and blessings. We are the elephant, and we bring with us the joy of the great breath of healing.

Our lungs are enormous. To walk on this land in such large forms we must have enormous lungs. We allow ourselves great in-breathes of healing. We share much with the Earth. We give, in Light and love, the communal healing necessary for our tribe. And we would like, at sometime in the future, to share healing with those of the human species, but at this time we are distanced by the fear, greed, and desire for power which permeates human life.

Now, at least, we can share with you some common ground in the process of healing. We rely, as you do, upon the same angelic spirits that govern the process of healing for all the infirm, whether animal, vegetable, or mineral. So we know what it is to heal. We must, in fact, heal everyday. Sometimes the task seems too daunting, as our numbers are diminishing. Our range has been so curtailed by human overpopulation and growth, that we can tell you we are fearful we will become extinct. But, in fact, we know that the Earth is going through significant transformations now, and we have confidence in our Creator God, that no harm is to come to our kind. Extinction is not the extinction of souls, but, nevertheless, it can produce misgivings in everyone. If you do not understand, then please step back a little bit from your human point of view. You believe that you are the dominant species of the planet, and this thought is a curse on your kind. It could be that you are dominating yourselves out of existence, more so than we. It could be that you are creating more sickness for yourself in your desire to control, than we are in our sub-servience to God's will and our readiness to share.

Be that as it may, we want to give you some aid in your own healing, as we are beings of Light and love ourselves. Whatever happens, the healing process must be seen in its detail, discipline must be used, and some tenacity must be acquired. We are not at this point concerned with how you are working through the healing, but that you are willing to heal. You have taken on some healer as a guide, for they are only guides. You have applied some diligent effort to your own healing process or to the healing process of others, if you are another's guide. Here you see yourself day after day working towards healing, and asking God whether there will be an end to what you do to heal. It seems as if healing is endlessly ongoing. It seems as if, in the demand for everyone to heal in love, that healing must be taken on forever, or that you are just asking for it redundantly. God is hearing you, but, at the same time, persistently allowing pain to come to you or another. You become frustrated at this vicious cycle of healing and illness and healing again. And you begin to ask yourself, in judgment of God, whether you should just slack off or throw up your hands and walk away saying that if you are to heal at all, you must heal instantly.

We can say to you that you are much in need of letting loose your judgment of God. You are not eternally plagued by the darkness in and around you. It is not simply that you are being tortured by a god who is half dark and half Light. Neither are you being pestered by a world which is part in darkness and part in Light. Rather, you are acquiring a new ability to heal, and you are raising yourself up inch by inch. It would be better to say you are unfolding self—discarding the old self, and embracing a more noble self each time you do healing. You do not plateau after a healing, but reach a new level through the force of Light from what has been healed. Feeling as if you have always been on this level, you seek some forward progress and find something that needs yet to be healed in you. And, in healing, you enable the old self to shed and a new self to rise to yet another level. But, because this process goes on for long periods of time, you tend to forget what you are doing, and how you are learning, and how you are evolving.

What is it that so impels you to make forward progress? Is it the desire of the soul to be better, to sit in pride and thumb its nose at others who are not in such a lofty position? No, it is the desire to raise the expression of your essence to that of God, knowing wherever and however God is, and whatever the essence of God truly is, that you will never fully be able to be God yourself. Rather, you will be able to raise yourself to a greater level of expression and oneness with this essence.

You must understand that if you depart from this process of evolving, you will fall into darkness. Love demands movement all of the time, and demands that you take with you all that is of love which you have won in the past. Nothing of love dies. As high a position as you may reach, you do not shed love, but you shed self, shed self's artifacts, and shed darkness.

It seems that you would find yourself in an interminable process. But, we say to you that the soul's evolution cannot be held up, and you cannot rise to your highest level because you have no highest expression of soul. We also say that you have no highest level of self. This evolution is a process of joy and love.

Rise above your narrow perception of being on this healing treadmill, and say to yourself that you only move in joy, and your passage through creation is an evolutionary one, and you need not seek an endpoint. Your goal is nonexistent, and you need to say this to yourself with the greatest self love you can muster.

My message is one, in essence, of patience. Without patience, the joy in your spiritual growth will be sucked out of you. You will find yourself on a treadmill of healing, running around over and over, going through the same territory, wondering why you are not healed, or wondering why, after you heal one disease, another arises to be healed. While you are still in disease, whether it is disease of the body, heart, or mind, remember that there comes a time for all disease to end. The cycle of life, death and rebirth is not the cycle of taking on, coping with, and dispelling disease. If you decide to depart from this

Earth with a pattern of disease, you will rejoin this Earth with a developed pattern of disease, and you will acquire disease again. Your healing does not stop just because your body is dead. As the source of your healing power lies in your ability to heal in the present, you always will have the ability to heal, and you always must heal what is given to heal or it will relentlessly chase you.

Your need for patience is not set in the void, nor in any nihilistic space. It is rather set in the promise that all things which need to be healed will be healed. It is not a particular pact between God and you which enables this. It is rather your desire to evolve as a soul which will cause the inception and the cessation of all disease. You take on disease in order to heal it. And you heal in order to evolve. Whatever you think you need to heal will come to an end—then you will find that there is more work to do. But as you evolve, you will see this work becoming of a lighter and lighter nature, and dark things will pass from you with facility.

You do not need to take on heavy burdens in order to mature in spirit. The saints of the world did not seek out disease and pain in order to bring healing to themselves or others. They simply lived in this world, conscious that they could not escape suffering. At the same time, they were conscious that all suffering comes to an end. Whether it ends in one life or another is the purview of God, and not of those who dwell on the Earth. You must have patience in order to allow joy to emerge. You are a being who can excite those lively centers of your body to allow healing to flow through all that is your self at the moment.

We animal beings of this Earth will not withdraw from our mutual healing. We have healing to do for you of the human species, and you have healing to do for us. We are beings of love, and yet we are not immune to hardship. All suffering calls forth healing, however a healing governed by love, and not by suffering itself. Please refrain from calling suffering upon yourself in your impatience to heal. Do not plead to God from a position of suffering, because then you will have reinvested in the self as one who suffers, and you will undo the healing which has already taken place in you. As soon as you recognize the need for healing and accept God's healing power, healing is being done. Do not disconnect yourself from this healing force because your suffering is calling out for release.

If you allow the force of love to call forth healing, you will find that you will be healing in lighter and lighter stages until the process of taking on disease is something that is Light. Suffering then, loses its substance, and darkness releases its grip on you. Do not allow yourself to wallow in self-pity. The suffering self may end up being a self which can be very tenacious. Your identity with your own suffering, through your lack of patience with God, may cause you to invest energy into this false self that will, in turn, cause your death. Your true self is one of love and beauty. See this and remember that you, also, are here to learn.

We of the animal realm seem to bear our suffering with dignity. We attempt, at least on a subconscious level, to be noble in our dealings with our own pain and disease, whether it is of our hearts, our minds, or our bodies. It is not instinct which causes us to sit patiently with our healing process and suffer without crying out. It is our soul's acknowledgment that healing can only take place through love and by identifying with love and not fear or suffering. We of the elephants, massive as our bodies are, must have that much more patience, for we are pestered by many small creatures around us, wanting to invade out of darkness. There is darkness around us, just as there is darkness around human beings. As huge as we are, we are that much more susceptible to disease. We can tell you that our trials will only end when we join together and use the force of our love, our Light energy, to heal the whole planet again.

If you believe, as you walk through this world, that you have a period of time when you are free of problems, and you cannot focus on where healing is needed for anyone, remember the Earth. She is even more immense than we are. And she has many small entities upon her who are pestering her and giving her disease. When you can find no one around you whom you believe needs healing, stop and give healing to the Earth. She will always respond in love. There is no place we see upon this Earth that does not need some healing. Do not forget your sister. We know what it is like to be large and to be beset by darkness. In your compassion, seek out all those who are in need and share your healing gifts with them.

We depart from you now in love. Good-bye.

Jesus

⬤ The Sixth Gate

This is Jesus. My friends, I come to you for the first time in this book to speak to you about the end of healing and the beginning of life. As all life comes from the process of healing, everything which has been created is in need of constant response, the reinvestment of thought and heart in order to maintain creation. There is no creation beyond God's mechanism of birth and rebirth. God's response to all of creation is to heal, and in healing, to create anew. Renewed creation is the greatest healing possible. It is healing directly from God. As we see the world from God's eyes, we see it in terms of its needs and wants, what it loves and what it detests, and so, we bring healing to it. As you have learned to be a creator, you must respond to what you have created. God's passion to create demands healing, and as it does, creation is renewed.

You can go all over the world and find many varied techniques for healing. I did not remain in my lifetime in the simple place in which I was born. Rather, I traveled the world in search of the perfect healing for the mind, heart, body, and soul. We searched and searched, and yet we could not find it. We looked high and low. We looked across the sea. We looked beyond the seas and over the mountains. Yet, we could not see what our hearts told us was most necessary to give in our lives.

The notion that in my life I had an immediate sense of purpose is not true. I had to come to my sense of purpose. I had to come to my senses, also. And I had to explore and discover. You can say that throughout this book there has been nothing but exploration and discovery.

You might think that, in the process of trying to heal oneself or another, if there is a difference, you must find just the right methodology. But, this cannot be. There is no one right method. There is no esoteric healing ritual. There is no secret scientific formula. There are no sacred herbs tucked away somewhere in a monastery. There is no amulet which will bring release from pain or protection from the darkness. There is only one healing. This one healing may manifest itself in many forms, as the One Soul manifests itself in many bodies. Nevertheless, it is one healing. And the end of your journey towards healing is an end of your exploration and discovery.

The last stage to which you come in healing is where you are most in contact with this Oneness, where you have put aside all the machinations of self—whether you believe that you are the healer or the healed, and whether you know where you give healing. You have already employed one healer or another. You have had patience with your process. You know where the Light is, and where the darkness is, and you embrace the Light. Now, in this last stage, all these things become trivial. They become so, not by your desire to be superior or to transcend, but by your wish not to transcend, because, when healing, you cannot transcend. In the course of healing, this would only be denial. In this last gate you have put aside all things as trivial except for your desire for contact with God. This One God does not blink or shed a tear, but keeps an open eye; She sees you and never stops seeing you; She loves you and never stops loving you; She has created you and is willing to help recreate you, as you respond to the self who is created and as you wish a new self.

As the old self becomes decrepit, you call out to God, not to me or to another healer. You finally call out to God in the body and ask for healing. You ask with abandonment. Have you not noticed that we did not make the plea to God the first gate of healing? No, it is instead the last threshold you must cross. And this last gate is the recognition that there is only one healer, and that is God.

And it is this recognition that calls you to petition, to beg, to pray to God for healing. Without this prayer there is no contact. It may be a wonder that God enthroned witnesses you, but up until now your back has been to this God. And you have not felt to be in His favor enough to turn about, even if it was to kneel, or to humble yourself before Him. You have not felt the urge to turn around and face your Creator. Why? You believed that you must heal yourself first to be worthy enough to face God. So, how could you therefore ask healing from Him? And yet, we say this is your final step without which you cannot proceed into healing. Once you proceed in this manner, all other steps are unimportant and become moot.

We can speak from our own experience as a human being that your feeling you can turn toward God only when you have purified yourself by healing is very human. And as a human being desperately wanting to be perfect or fine or beautiful or holy, you have withdrawn from God, not wanting to present an unholy aspect of yourself to Him. You have kept your eyes from your Creator, until you have gotten so desperate that you have at last kneeled and humbled yourself, or cringed and awakened yourself, or cowered and cast your eyes down. But you have faced the Creator at last, because all the patience and all the practice in the world have done you no good. You are still ill. If you are not ill in the body, you are ill in the mind, or you are ill in the heart. And you know that if you have discharged some form of darkness from you, it will come back, because something is yet not right. It is only in your facing the Creator and allowing yourself to be one with the Creator that you can heal.

This last gate is one of confrontation. It describes why you have gotten so low. Through it you will deliver yourself into a heightened state. What has caused you not to face the Father, not to pray to the Father? Is it vanity? Is it agnosticism? Is it hatred of a Creator who has made a world in which there is suffering? Is it judgment of yourself, or judgment of God?

It is none of these things, my friend, but rather it is you believe you have needed to seek justice, and therefore you needed to seek a righteous god. And so this righteous god needs its minions to justify itself. This false god, this idol to whom you pray, or to whom you seek to justify yourself, is a dark god, but it is an idol whose face is ubiquitous. You see the god of justice all around you. "You will be judged upon your death." "Only those souls who have led a good life will be brought into heaven." "Unless you beg for forgiveness you will not find god, or find peace in paradise."

The god of justice is asking you to heal yourself. This false idol that weighs and judges every soul, this thing of darkness, is not your God. Your God is a God of mercy and of love. Your God is a God of compassion. All healing is a return to the compassion with which you have begun your journey. All healing is a loosening of your bonds to compassion and a rebinding to that compassion. All healing is a discovery of a lost God, the True God, the God of love and compassion, who cannot keep His eyes off you and holds you in His embrace at all times. You say to yourself, "I am small. I am humble. I am in pain. I have many sins. I have strayed." We have tried to tell you many times, please forgive yourself, for we have a forgiving God.

You have turned in some way away from God, seeking justification for yourself somewhere out there, in the ether. You have cast your heart into the void, hoping it will fishhook some self justification, and it will not. You have turned your eyes somehow away from God, and you have needed healing. And, in turning your eyes back toward God, you find that you are healed by compassion and that this healing is instantaneous and complete. The just god cannot heal. The just god cannot love, because the just god places justice above all things. The True God heals, is compassionate, and has forgotten justice, even if He has spent millennia in determining what is justice and what is not. In God's moment of compassion He forgets all righteousness.

You do not have to justify your position to God, because there is no way you can do it. This is not your place. Ultimately, you would have to justify your very existence. But you have not created your existence, so you cannot. Even if God takes the time to find what the route of justice is, this is abandoned in the first instant He faces you. The Father God confronts you in love and compassion. Justice is split asunder and dissolves in the void, for God cannot hold you in His eyes without love. And you have this moment to say to yourself that you believe in God enough to turn back toward Him in love. If you bow and scrape or if you turn in pride, if you have benevolence or if you turn in lust and greed, if you are humble or if you turn hungry for power, if you are pure or if you turn deceitful, as long as you turn towards God, you will receive God's grace.

The God without justice is the God who holds grace. You do not perceive God holding up scales, blindfolded. Have you noticed that your imagery of what is justice is most appropriate to our dialogue? Here is justice that is blind, that will not look upon you. It will not see you in love nor see you as an individual nor see you as God's creation. It knows you not at all but feels only the balance of justice. It offers the sword of punishment, of conviction.

The God who sees you must see you in compassion. The God who has created must respond to the world in love and must hold every being ultimately in compassion and cannot be blind. You cannot restore your connection to God, because you have not lost it. If you had lost it, you would cease to be. You cannot find the understanding of your connection to God, because it is endless and you cannot understand that which is infinite. But you can remember, because, in disease, you have forgotten. You can recall that you have come from God, that you are God's child, and that you are healed through God. Instead, if you choose to say, "Look at this marvelous healing I have done on myself, or my doctor has done on me, or my friends have done on me, or my psychologist has done on me," even if you say, "Look what I have done from Your creation," you will be facing the void. Instead of attempting to justify yourself to God, if you turn toward God from the point in which you are now, emotionally and physically, and accept God, and ask God for healing, you will receive grace. God's grace flows freely from the fountain that is the heart of the universe and is in the heart of the Godhead. It is an endless fount of miracles. You simply must turn to it. You must do this without hesitation. You must do it from where you are and not from where someone else is, or from the hope of yourself to be.

You are healed by God's grace alone. All other healing is impossible. So, why not turn to God's grace now and accept it? You have been doing without it for such a long time, that it seems as if you are trying to prove a point. Is it that, if God is alive, then He must prove it? Or, if God is dead, then you must make do? Or is it that God loves you as much as another, or loves you less, or loves you more?

Are you ready for God? Are you prepared? Have you done the sacraments? Have you cleansed yourself? There are many people on the Earth for whom you must dress properly before you entertain to be in their presence. You must have purified and cleansed your body of dirt and odor. You must give them a resume or a letter of introduction. You must speak to them on the phone or make an appointment with their secretary. You must prepare your heart and your mind to meet these people, but this is not God. All the preparation which you make for knowing or appreciating God's grace will bring you nowhere. You simply must turn and face your Creator. Be willing to do this even if you feel abject pride, or self-loathing. God's grace flows willingly, freely and endlessly out into the universe. It is unimaginably beautiful and complete. It is that part of God which is the response to what has already been created. It is not the original force of creation itself, but it is the force of ongoing creation. It is the force of God's loving response.

The Father does not see you, my friends, in judgment and does not see you in anger, but sees you in love. The Father is as loving as the Mother. The Mother God wishes to nourish and protect her children, and the Father God wishes likewise. There is nothing you need or can do to justify yourself to God. The only response there can be in love is acceptance.

If God's grace is pervasive, what is the point of directing hearts and minds to the Creator? The point is that unless you receive God's grace individually, it will not come at all to you. Banish the god of justice within you. This is a god unworthy of you. It is a god who cannot hold you in love. The God who is willing to create you is willing to heal you, and healing is creation anew. The God willing to create you is willing to continue creation. That is God's grace, and from the heart of God it flows to you, but you must receive it.

My friends, all of us who have walked the Earth have had troubles, have needed healing and have wanted to accept it. We have asked for God's forgiveness. It is not that we need to ask for God's forgiveness because we have sinned or strayed, or because we need to redeem ourselves, or because someone else needs to redeem us. We do not need to ask for forgiveness to open this gate to the reception of God's grace, for God has already forgiven us, my friends. It is that we need to turn our face to God. If you ask for forgiveness, you will find a God who has already forgiven you, who knows nothing but forgiveness, and whose heart is so great that there is nothing you can do to separate yourself from Him. It is the God of infinite love who creates infinite healing.

I wish I could say there were some esoteric technique that, once learned, would cause all healing to be possible, and all trials, false starts, and failures to be eliminated. But, I cannot. I have searched and I have found that this goal was an empty one. It is only your relationship to God which enables healing. It is only because there is a loving God, a God who has already forgiven you, a God of infinite compassion and mercy, a God who produces infinite grace that you can heal. It is only your relationship with God which calls forth healing.

At all times, behind everything is the force of God. If you cannot accept Him directly, God will work through one individual after another, perhaps even myself. You will go to one doctor or another, or you will be one practitioner after another. All of the time, God's grace pours through those whose heart intent has given them the freedom to pass healing through them. Ultimately, you must come to terms with what is behind the mask of self, the God who is behind all things, the Source underlying all. The contemplation that you come to God through healing is the awareness of God's grace.

God's grace is forgiveness. It is compassion. It is mercy. It is healing. It disdains ego. It disdains justice. It disdains judgment. It disdains fear. It asks nothing of you, but loves you just for being alive. Whether you have accomplished an enlightened feat of compassion, or you have lived in squalor and hatred, it is all the same. God's grace will be there for you in as great a magnitude.

You do not need to search out this God who is with you at all times. You need only to turn and face Him. If you ask, "Why is this person healing and I am not?" you are not facing God. Rather, if you rejoice in what you have and who you are, you can find that there is more of God's grace pervasive in the universe than you can believe.

I have spoken enough. I leave you now with my love and my blessings for you and all of my friends. Good-bye.

PART THREE

Transcendence

Preface

We bring you greetings from the Source of all Light and Love. This is Lenonda. We are most pleased to be able to speak to you at this juncture. In Part Three you are going to examine the steps to transcendence. This part is not transcendence itself, and you may feel as if we have left you off a little abruptly at the doorstep of your transcendence, but this is not a door through which we can also cross.

You, having sought out creation, compassion and healing, now need to understand the nature of what healing is bringing to you. We have been speaking to you as beings in the body. After all, the book is directed toward those who are incarnate and not those who are dead or on other planes. In this book you can see that everything has some manifestation in the body; everything takes form in the material world. And how you understand the material world and yourself determines how you understand your soul and all aspects of self.

With your permission, we would like to continue with the exploration of the spirit's expression through the body. You have a number of layers of self, do you not? You have a mind that is able to transcend the mere body. You have feelings which you know you carry from lifetime to lifetime. And you have a soul that is so inexorably linked to other souls that it is difficult to speak of yourself as an individual. All these facets of you converge in body, or shall we say, since you are incarnate, all these facets of you can be perceived and studied through body. It is the body that takes the first step in understanding and not the mind. The teaching of the elders in your society is that the baby takes its first step before it solves its first riddle or completes its first abstract thought. So, the first step of any spiritual process is a body step. We have thus taken you on a mountain journey which has enabled you to determine that you must go within the mind, and then, having gone within, walk out into the world anew and make your way through it in a truly spiritual manner. But because we are not speaking to disembodied spirits, it is fitting that whatever your goal may be in this lifetime, even the goal of transcendence, you must take on the task of reaching this goal in the body. You cannot lay body aside without suffering.

We will take you in this part to the first step of transcendence. But we will leave you there. It is not our place to cross over with you, for we cannot show you what is on the other side and will not pretend as if we know what it is already. Is this, in a manner of speaking, to say that everyone's transcendence is different? No. Everyone's transcendence is the same, but everything which leads up to it is unique. The body is your guide at this point to reach transcendence. It has always been so. To deny body is to create fear of it and disease in it, and we would not recommend this as a course. You will quickly revert to suffering in an attempt to escape from body. Denial does not work.

Where has healing brought you? Has it brought you to the realization that there is no further healing to be done? Well, it cannot. If love is infinite and in constant demand of healing, healing must also be infinite. The infinite power of healing is also an infinite impetus to heal. Does the healing say that you are unworthy? We believe that we have taken you through some steps that have enabled you to see that you are not unworthy. The healing, being infinite, is enabling you to evolve in body, in mind, in soul and in feelings. So, we take you now to the next step which this infinite healing would suggest. It may not be a step you are ready to accept, but it must be accepted. In fact, your acceptance up until now has been a kind of wrestling with self where you have been overcoming the duality between who does the healing and who is healed—who gives, and who receives. Now, a new duality gets expressed to you, so that you may overcome it.

We bid you adieu. We will return, of course. Go forward with our blessings.

The First Gate

We bring you greetings from the Light of Christ which Jesus has given to this world. We are, my friends, humble beings like you. We have no decorations, no diplomas. We have no special skills. We have no inordinate mark. We are not angelic beings. We do not swim with the fish or fly with the owl. We are simply alive in this world with you, or we soon will be. We are beings of love.

As you sit and listen or read, know that for some time I have sat, perhaps much like you, and I have watched the world go by with my own corporeal eyes and wondered what the nature of God was and how healing was ever to take place.

You have seen that the infinite love of God which has been brought to you has demanded that God's grace must heal and be experienced every moment. There can be no time, whether it is a moment of pain or joy, of reluctance or spontaneity, of calm or agitation, of love or a time when disdain is felt on your tongue like a bitter remedy, when grace cannot be called forth directly from God Himself.

You could believe that you are separate in body from God. But as God's grace comes to you, this ability to feel tells you that there is no such thing, that God is joined with you in your struggle to be alive, that you do not just bear God within you, for that would not be enough. It is that God is yet empowering you, nourishing you, sustaining you, and joining with you.

You can go through life seeking healing and not caring at all who is to be healed. Is it yourself or another? You cannot know. But you can become quite adjusted to the thought that this grace of God permeates the universe and that you can call upon its power at any time. As you do, you find that openings are made. As a man with great riches who lives in a palace finds many doors to open, the doorways to the riches of the Father bring the comforts and joy of friendship, the comforts of food, drink and shelter, the comforts of abundance, which are now in your grasp, for abundance from the Father is as if at your fingertips.

With this knowledge, you could go with great confidence into the world as a child who is assured of his inheritance. Healing would then be a dog who comes when you snap your fingers. Love would transport you through the world. This Light of the Christ would sustain you, drive you and empower you. You beg to ask us, "Is there any more to life than this?" We would have to say there is no more, except that your mind is still held in a duality, and your release must be imminent.

I sit before you. You can walk through this world like a prince or a princess and in doing so, find yourself before one such as me. You stare at me. Your jaw drops, perhaps. I may spoil your sense of a Loving Father God. I may shake your understanding of what creation, love and healing have been about, but I myself will not be unsettled. I will not move because, immovable, I am your vehicle for transcendence. I will not move because I cannot walk. I am disabled. I have always been disabled, and I may be disabled in another life. No longer attached to thoughts of self, you have begun in compassion to accept that all is bound by love and the Oneness of all things. But sitting here, my legs unable to stir, I challenge your perception.

What great healer has found me? Not one has. Though I may exist in many forms, I am yet in this other form for you. You realize when you see me, that I have come into this body at least for you. You witness me as a crippled being, because you come from this direct contemplation of the Father. You have been delivered by your willingness to embrace the Father, and with sufficient strength and healing, you are set to go about the world. But, you see, here I am, the first being whom you meet.

I have been waiting for you here in my chair, immovable. You realize quickly that you have come to me, for I could not have come to you. I must be your next appointment. As we stare at each other, you are reminded of facing the Father. I am your brother. We speak without exchanging words. I am unable to move. All the Light and all the grace in the universe will not stir my legs. Do I tell you this? No, you tell me this.

Then do I wail and moan? You become frightened at the prospect that I will not. You are shaken to the bone. For, all this time, you have been concerned about who heals and who does not heal and you have not confronted what heals and what does not heal, or what is and what is not.

We believe you will come closer. You desire to touch. We see this. You are not pushed forward by thought, because thought is telling you that to touch me will be useless. It is the feeling of compassion which blossoms within you again, as compassion must. You come to me, and you touch my leg. Perhaps you fumble for some coins. I do not ask for them. I am not a beggar. I will shake my head. I will not accept them. Your lips part and an utterance begins to rise from your throat. I cut it short with my eyes. There is nothing you can say to me. You cannot escape the knowledge that I will not heal in this lifetime. This knowledge has no educator and yet is deeply felt.

My friend, I did not know this until you told me. I had forgotten. But you have touched my legs regardless. And somehow my lifeless legs have become like antennae for something that I was not sure existed until I met you. You have been willing to give anyway. And I am now receiving. I cannot tell you what this means to me. My legs are alive and vital in a way that may be unimaginable to you. It certainly has been unimaginable to me. Here I had thought that they were, at least for the moment, dead and useless. But somehow, in your touching, I have felt God's grace come to me. In fact, these limp limbs seem better at receiving grace than any of my whole parts.

And I am grateful. You have accepted me, and in acceptance you say that you do not care what can be healed, or what cannot be healed. Your compassion has driven you to the realization that you do not know what is to be healed when you attempt healing. You know that healing comes from God and is His grace. And your willingness to touch my legs, is a willingness to accept that you do not know what is to be healed and what is not to be healed, for God's grace has not given you God's omniscience. You are driven by compassion to overcome the duality of what is to be healed and what is not. Healing is the drive of compassion put into action. You are willing to manifest this.

How many others have passed me by, thinking that they know what is and what is not? They did not want to disturb me. They thought they knew what could be healed and what could not. They wanted to leave me in peace with that awareness. They were not able to speak this out of shame, pity and a lack of grace. But grace has come to you and told you that you need to come to me and make this offering. Now I feel it in my crooked legs. I feel what I had not felt before. And, truly, I feel something must be healed, or else there is no grace. This must be grace. Truly something must be healed, but I have no idea what it is, any more than you.

Forced to sit here, I must accept. But you know that through the efforts of your own two legs you have been transported to me. You are blessed in this, my friend. If there has not been any other deed that you have committed which has been worthy of yourself or of God, this one has. If you needed to be saved, you have now saved yourself. And, I now can feel. But where I feel or how I feel is of no importance. You have given me that.

You can proceed forward bearing this gift you have given yourself out of a love which had no precepts or borders. It was not in anger or in resignation that you sought the acceptance to overcome this duality. It was love and the pull to heal which brought you to acceptance. You could have been another who came to me and said, "I will heal you." And I would have felt nothing. In all the methods and machinations of your attempt, I would have received nothing. But you were not driven by ego, and you did not seek non-attachment. You simply experienced acceptance in love and were driven by it to touch and to heal. And this has brought some healing —to where, I do not know— but I feel it.

We cannot have prepared you for this stage. Realize it was thrust upon you, but it is your First Gate. We would have lied to you if we had said you had to work for us, because you could not work for us. Effort in non-attachment is effort wasted. There can be no effort in acceptance. One either accepts or does not. My love and gratitude is with you. Though I am human, sometimes, I feel like a small animal in a world of giants. You have made me feel human again. I am grateful, both like a human who walks upon two legs, and like a cripple who must slither along the ground.

Good-bye, and God bless you.

The Walrus

● # The Second Gate

We welcome you to the Second Gate of transcendence. We are powerful beings; we are not weak ones. We do not go forth in creation with trepidation, or without feeling the warmth of our own body, even in the cold of the harshest environment. We are beings of great heart—our hearts beat to circulate blood through great bodies. We have listened to the speech of this human who has come before, and we are not saddened by him, nor do we lapse into pity. Instead, we understand the need to accept what is in the world in Light and in dark, and what is healed and what seems not to be healed, although, these things do not always show themselves in the light of truth.

I work in the depths as you work in the depths. You are not on the highest plane of existence. Being bound to the Father, and then receiving from the Father, does not mean that you work in the high realms of the universe. You are not trapped in this realm, but the pressure of it may be greater than you give it credit. You cannot avoid the fact that your own body is strong and powerful and full of heart, and yet is subject to disease and in need of healing. It is this reality that I show you. I am a being of the depths. I am a being who works in pressure where the light of the sun is dim.

We are the walrus. We have our own way of living in dignity. We are as crippled as the man on the chair, because our legs will not walk on the Earth one step at a time. We move by groveling. We grovel on land in imitation of the snake. But in the depths of the ocean we move with alacrity and speed. Here we become graceful, and our buoyant bodies are supple and elegant. Perhaps our friend in some way is able to navigate through life in a manner you cannot imagine, or you cannot dream for yourself. Is this possible? Do I have legs which take me across land easily? I do not. And yet I breathe air.

Here I am in the water, an air-breather. The water is most comforting. Its cold does not bother me. I even have ways to defend myself. How is one to know the purpose of life? Do you know? If you seek not to be attached, if you acquire acceptance, do you understand purpose, therefore? I show you my purpose. Will that bring you enlightenment? My purpose, it seems to me, is to go down into the depths of the ocean, to record the movement of the land under the surface of the water, and to harmonize living beings with this knowledge.

Are you content that I have shared this with you? Are you enlightened by this dialogue? I do not think so. If you knew the purpose of a man being disabled, or of a great being such as myself who breathes air living more contentedly in the water, would that bring you enlightenment? I do not think so. The tale of our own folklore says that God Herself becomes dim when we plunge into the depths of the sea. You would think that this would be a horrible experience, and yet down where the light is dim we find our greatest fulfillment. You have not really accepted that some things can be healed and some things cannot be. You do not even know whether this is true. You must have acceptance that you know or you believe you know some things and you cannot know or believe you cannot know other things. Acceptance is just that. You do not know what can be healed and what cannot be healed; you cannot see what you have imagined you must understand in order to survive. If clinging to self brings up anything, clinging brings up the fear of the ignorance of what must be, or of what can be, or of what cannot be, or of what the purpose of everything or anything is.

We are willing to work where the light is dim. We are simply willing to experience. We find, in fact, that dimness is the moment of our greatest pleasure. We rejoice as we experience it.

You have made a mistake in understanding your own acceptance. Your acceptance could not have been for what is and what is not, because truly the light is too dim for you to see what is and what is not. It is acceptance of your lack of knowing. It is acceptance that whatever comes in sight is dim, as if seen through murky waters. Although you see light and cannot see anything but light, this light is not always the most radiant. Do you recall when the light of the sun was most starkly brilliant? It was when you were experiencing emptiness. We know this also. It is as if we could fly to the sun, and when we got there, God would show only emptiness to us.

Our fulfillment is to be in the Earth, in her waters, living and reaping enlightenment from it. The world will spin away from you the more you try to contemplate it. You are the only thing that does not pass like debris in the frigid waters of the sea of life.

We are proud, and we are strong. We do not suffer in the way you could imagine the suffering of a dumb animal. We find pleasure and fulfillment in all we do.

We have spoken too long and must get back to the business of our lives. We leave you with our blessing. Thank you. Go with God.

The Third Gate

We welcome you to the Third Gate. It is a gate of silence and repose. It is a gate of rejoicing and a gate of fruitful understanding. It is a gate where you meet me again, and where we establish our bonds. We have bonds to many beings. Who is to say where the strongest bond is? We do not know. I am the Archangel Gabriel. We are the angel of those who would give themselves to being born. We work with you, born into body. We work with you to make you understand what it is which compels you to be in the body.

You have gotten many lectures in spirit. Much dialogue takes place between you and your birth mother and father, between you and your guides and angels, and between you and your friends, before birth. Why would you contemplate such a foolish thing as to be in the body? You see before you a world that you cannot help but interpret as full of hardship and pain, and yet you are driven to be in the body in this world. What is wrong with you? You must have a copious desire for pain and suffering to be alive here. What have you done to yourself? As much as we have spoken to you and tried to get you to think about what you have done, you have rushed ahead and become born anyway. We had an obligation, a joyful one even, to help you be born, and we are grateful to have done so, but you have forgotten our dialogue. So, we now send you this little missive. Will it spark a remembrance? Hopefully, it will.

Where have you put your receipt for body? As if you have been to a store and purchased a body, you have a receipt. But, where have you put it, and why have you misplaced it? Is it in your shirt pocket? Is it in your pants? Have you encoded it onto a crystal computer chip and stuck it in some organ or gland? Where have you put it?

What could it mean to be walking the Earth without your receipt? What is written on the receipt? Is it that you have paid money to God for such a magnificent body which carries you so readily through this creation? No, you have not paid a single cent for it. You have not paid for it in blood, sweat or tears. Perhaps, your mother has, but you have not. Have you paid for it in chunks of soul which you now leave scattered throughout the universe and for which you are pining away? No, you have not left that either. Is it part of your mind which you now must recapture, because you cannot live in such a small, degraded body for long? Are you are aching to be the bigger being whom you know you are in heart? But, no, it is not that either. What is on the receipt? Is it how many lungs you will have, or how many eyeballs? You would not need a receipt for that. You could count those things, even lungs. What is on the receipt is your purpose. You have forgotten your purpose. It was written down for you. After chiding you about wanting to be alive, we and all those beings of whom we have spoken have persisted with you, so that you would know exactly what you are setting out to do in this life and exactly what your purpose is. Ignorantly you have lost the receipt.

When you look at the world by the dimness of the light and see, in murky detail, creation all around, you sit and wonder what its purpose is. You sit and think, "I wish that I knew. I wish that I could overcome this duality concerning why some things seem to be known to me and some things seem not to be." Directing this thought out into the world, you then look at the world and say, "Why? What is the meaning of life?" If we were to come back to you and say, "Well, you are the Creator God, make a meaningful purpose for life." You would come back to us shrunken and disheveled after weeks and months of ponderous thought, having come up with absolutely nothing. Why? You have lost your receipt. The world has no meaning until you have meaning. Unless you remember what meaning you have, you cannot hope to bring purpose into the world. So, what purpose do you have? Where is your receipt? Your purpose is written down. We have given it to you to hold, and now you have misplaced it. Please check your coat pocket. I do not think it is there, but check it anyway.

What are you to do, at this point, having lost your receipt? You must proceed forward in the realization that duality is being further broken down. Now, it is not the duality of what is and what is not; it is not the duality of what you know exists and what you do not know exists. It is now what is outside you and what is within you. If you search for meaning beyond you, you will return the empty fool. If you are the God who manifests everything, and if anything that you have manifested has meaning, then you, therefore, must have meaning, because you cannot have given that essence without having it yourself. If you have meaning, the Father must have meaning. If you understand your meaning, if you can pick up your receipt, you will have understood the Father's meaning. But the duality between yourself and the world, represented in meaning, is a most serious duality, and we cannot make light of it for long. You will torture yourself in the dimness of life in searching for meaning beyond yourself. So, cease it.

It is my observation that most pieces of paper in your world end up in trash receptacles. Could it be that you have trashed your meaning, thinking it was a self which you no longer needed? Or, could it be a new something which you have not imagined? This can give you pause to think. Nothing yet has seemed to be stable or rocklike. Everything seems to reveal itself to you in impermanence.

Perhaps you have the thought that you are a playwright. You follow a script, despite that you are actually writing it. Could it be that we have given you the receipt, but you are the one who has written on it?

We offer this thought to you and say good-bye from our heart and our soul. We are the ones who assisted you in being born. We might come to you to say, "Your purpose is finished in this life. It is time to go." In this dimness, the angel of birth and the angel of death may seem to be the same angel.

We depart from you with love and a tenderness for the fool who was willing to be born in love.

The Gazelle

◉ The Fourth Gate

Y ou can imagine what it would be like to go through the world with a true receipt. What self-judgment would be yours. How you would constantly want to search for God's justification and acceptance. And no matter how many times you hear the words that God has accepted you already and gives you love, you would be searching endlessly.

What you have done with your receipt, my friends, is deliberately lost it. You have not misplaced it. You have not put it aside for safekeeping. It is not locked up in a treasury or a vault. You have deliberately thrown it out. You have trashed it. Some man with a paunch, in dirty overalls and with grease on his well-worn gloves has picked up your receipt and thrown it into his shabby gray trash truck.

Where is your receipt? Well, you know very well what you have done with it. As soon as you learned to read, you threw it out. Do you remember the first ascent? You threw out your receipt before then. We believe it was thrown in the park and some squirrel was chewing on it. Then, the man who comes to pick up the trash in the park took it some time ago. You seem to be well sustained without it.

You want to know what your purpose is, so that you know what is and what is not, because what meaning tells you is what is and what is not. What does not have meaning does not need to be, and that which is meaningless is nonexistent. If you create the world, then you must have meaning, or else the world is devoid of meaning. If you have meaning, then God must have meaning. But, here you are, having ripped up your receipt, sustained, full of life, feeling the power of the Creator, compassion, and the urge to heal, and moving into stages that you do not yet understand. How could this be? Has our logic failed? Well, we have not attempted to make logic, not great logic, in any case. Does what needs to exist needs to have meaning in order to have existence? Between you and me, it probably does. But, could you know what this meaning is? In trying to make meaning elusive, are you playing a game with yourself?

You have thrown your receipt out. Everything which could be written was written on it. And, now, you are in doubt that anything at all was ever written on your receipt. But, should you go back and search? Where are you going to search? How are you going to get back? To which point are you going to return? You are now nowhere. You have worked your way out of one realm, whatever realm it was, and are nowhere.

You cannot work your way back home, my friends, to scour the debris of life for some meaning. What is there to do instead? Since it does not serve you to look back, it serves you only to look forward. Have you noticed that the selves you have discarded have not stacked themselves up into some kind of monumental edifice? You could not have scaled this edifice as you would a great pyramid. You have, rather, left selves behind you like so many turds in a field. And, in looking back, you see nothing of value to you.

We are speaking to you from the realm of animal. We are the gazelle. The gazelle moves quickly with grace and beauty. Grace is something you have sought and attained. Beauty of movement is something yet elusive to you. But, as you move, again and again, you realize that you have not been able to be still in any case.

Suppose you have written something profound on that receipt? If you had kept it with you, would it now have meaning for you? Could it have been the case that the fool was wiser than he appeared to be, even to yourself? If you had written something profound on the receipt and had kept it with you on your fool's journey, how would you see yourself now? You would have been held inexorably to that purpose. In discarding your receipt, you may have performed the greatest act of wisdom ever, since you would have failed in any purpose you put down. You could not have possibly succeeded. At least, you could not have succeeded in any given stage. We doubt you could have known what your path was, so we doubt you could have applied your meaning to it. Your meaning, after all, is circumscribed by the path you are on.

It could have been that, as a fool, you were incredibly wise to have put that receipt in the trash, but you have not appreciated this. We of the animal realm, in moving so lightly and rapidly through the world, cannot turn and look back. When we do, we are caught and killed. When we do, we lose the grace evident in our movement. It is the same grace that could be yours, as there is only one grace. We move in beauty without abandon. Whatever you have scribbled on your receipt is of no importance to us. We cannot read. It should be of no importance to you. Have you not assumed that you could have read it? Perhaps you could have at one point, but now you cannot, for so many selves have been played out of you. Perhaps the self who could have read the receipt is gone and you should not try to retrieve that self. Perhaps, if you held the receipt in your hand, it would be gibberish.

You are never to know meaning. It would require rest and contemplation. Whatever stops and contemplates self may end up getting eaten. When the gazelle moves forward, movement itself becomes meaning, and it is not the self's meaning.

Could meaning reside in being still? Now, if you search for meaning in your attempt to overcome duality, you have assumed that there is one meaning, or that meaning is fixed and cannot be transcended. You have assumed that meaning is God itself, that it is as immutable as the Godhead. The Father, rather, says, "I give you meaning, and tomorrow I will give you another meaning." The Father is not fixed on meaning. If you are overcoming duality, it is now time to create diversity. Why have you assumed instead that there is only one meaning, and that meaning has been set and is a given?

When you look to meaning in life, you do not move like a gazelle. A gazelle knows that every footstep has meaning or nothing has meaning. So, we are willing to shed self and to shed the meaning of self as we take each step. We do this in grace and in beauty.

My friends, it is difficult for us to speak without feelings of compassion for you, for you are not given many inherent gifts; you need to work for them. If we of the animal kingdom seem to laud over our gifts, we know they are just that — gifts. You must work hard for everything you do. Please do not blame yourself for being less than what you imagine you could be. You would, likewise, be rushing ahead of yourself and not see and understand that the best movement is created by a willingness to put each foot down with a feeling of permanence and purposefulness. We do not attempt to be elusive and move into the future with the thought that meaning lies ahead. We are content that we are moving with such alacrity, because we are willing to make each step very firm and very purposeful. If you look back, you might be devoured; if you look too far forward, you might fall. We gaze ahead, but our thoughts are one with the meaning of the moment. What has meaning for you is what you have at hand to deal with, and nothing else. What has meaning for you is that to which you give meaning. To stay in the present moment is the greatest joy and the easiest peace.

We thank you in love.

The Vine Deva

The Fifth Gate

We are the being who represents to you the Fifth Gate of transcendence. We thank you for your patience in waiting for us. Throughout this time you have been working hard, and, in the attempt to find a path through the maze of false meanings, you have, perhaps, lost yourselves. We come to you to help you.

We are the deva of all vines. We find our own way through a world of false meaning, until we rise into the light of the sun, the Light which comes from the Father, and we feel the grace of God. We do not attempt to know or to understand what we hold. We coil ourselves to it and work our way around it. We weave our own nature on the framework that another has made. If you could see yourself, you could see that the old self, having been discarded, is now the framework around which your new self is to wind. You are a being that does not yet know its own transcendent self, but has only to rely on what has grown up and what is dying. You rely on what is self and what may no longer be self, but know that you can ascend to some place using what is old and good to press against.

If this is all your creation, then you are entitled to go forth like a vine and to wrap yourself around everything. It is a wrapping in love, for it is an acceptance of what you have created for yourself. Would we make ourselves into a stout tree whose fine tip is stretched up into the sky, which holds itself before the eye of the Father's sun? In doing that we would need to make root deep in the Earth and so fix ourselves into her. And, when we found that self was something impermanent, and that we had invested with meaning what could not hold meaning, then we would fall. This next gate is one of understanding that everything you attempt to invest with meaning is unfit, untrue, and meaningless itself. If it had meaning, you would have to keep it out of a sense of compassion and love. But also, you would have to keep it out of a sense of what is true. But self had no meaning, so you discarded it.

Are you left in a desert? These old selves seem to have no meaning. For, no self can have meaning, and you are right in discarding them. You have not lost the receipt so much as you have decided that this one receipt is wrong, and so all receipts are wrong. You have not grabbed another out of the hand of God. When you climbed the mountain with self, you found yourself lost and empty, facing the void, and almost falling in. But, when you climb the self like a vine, then you find that you can reach the top and leaflike face the sun and the rays of God. Whatever gets built gets destroyed. Whatever you believe that you can invest with meaning, you destroy with meaning, for whatever is built up must be destroyed. This was never a probability or possibility—it was a necessity.

We climb the tree. We are not ourselves the tree. We weave until we reach the top, and when we see that the bottom has our same leaves upon it, we rejoice, realizing that we drew much energy when on the bottom. We wind our way through a transcendent state, and when we reach it, we work our way down again. Well, what else do vines do when they run out of material on which to hold? We bring ourselves into being only by being willing to move. But now, we move with the knowledge that where we move to and where we have moved from have no meaning. We make the journey, not as a fool, but as a being willing to experience beauty.

You say that a life devoid of meaning must be emptiness. No, emptiness is life full of purported meaning. Emptiness is life full of pain. If self can have no meaning, does God have meaning? Do you ask God to toss out meaning to you so that you will be mesmerized by the false images of meaning? God has no meaning and does not wish to indulge in meaning; God has no intent to deceive and will not deceive.

If we take the tree away and magically maintain our position and form, you will perceive the tree as if still there. We are taking shape by movement. And the Father, also, takes shape through movement, and by a willingness to move, since love and healing are also movement. The gazelle has understood that, but you have not. You have attempted to root yourselves and to meditate. But, what is there on which to meditate? Whatever you have to contemplate will move like sand through your fingers. There is nothing to contemplate. All of your meditations have been like this, watching sand run through your fingers. Something had to flow when you decided to be rigid and stay still. The sands of thought moved. If your thoughts are in constant motion, they must be impermanent—and what is so impermanent cannot have fixed meaning.

Can you have completeness without meaning? You most certainly can. Are you not complete now? Is there not love around you, and in you? Is there not compassion in and all around you? Are you not attempting now, even as you are reading, to heal? Could this not be a sign that you are deserving of taking another breath, growing another leaf, and winding your way upwards? What could happen when you reach the top? Well, you could go back to the bottom. What is the harm if you go back to the bottom? There is no harm, this still is you.

We thank you for your patience. It has taken us quite some time to wind around. It seems that we labor greatly at everything we do. Yet we move with as much grace as the gazelle.

We thank you.

The Sixth Gate

We greet you at the entrance to the sixth and the final gate of transcendence. This is Lord Buddha. We are here by the request of the many souls who have asked for guidance from us and by our love and compassion, which enables us to speak through vast distances and impermeable dimensions. Are we to instruct you in transcendence? We cannot. We have resigned ourselves to the impossibility of speaking from one position to another, as if from that other position. We are resigned that, to speak from the place of transcendence to the place of wounded mortality and about that very transcendence, is impossible.

This, however, is no impediment to our dialogue. Lest it seem that we lack modesty, at least in part, we would wish to explain ourselves. Whether you have desired to be in a greater state, or you have desired that some aspect of self is in a greater state, you do not comprehend the who, what, where, why, and how of it. So, in seeking out one such as I, you also attempted to grab onto our cloak and perhaps share in that little bit of enlightenment we have. This is impossible, but perhaps not impossible for the reason you imagine. As you are moving into greater states of mind, and discharging thought forms which conflict you, you have forgotten something in the process. While we have talked to you about ascendancy, removing duality, overcoming attachment in acceptance, and moving to a place of contemplation where you are not concerned about meaning or self, we now tell you what you have forgotten. Transcendence is remembrance more than it is the acquisition of knowledge. It may not be a state to which you can take self. If there is no meaning and no self, what can guide or transport you there? You cannot create something when you are, likewise, in the process of stripping your self of meaning. You are not then in a position to do so. And if you stop and falsify a transcendent state, you will simply foil and confuse yourself.

It seems to be impossible for us to speak to you about transcendence when you are in such coarse, corporeal state. Yet, we do you a disservice when we do not. Which comes first, enlightenment or compassion? Compassion does. And in compassion, one seeks enlightenment. One does not find compassion through enlightenment. If you misunderstood me, I apologize, but it is impossible. It is another impossibility to conceive of enlightenment beyond a state of compassion. Many have made themselves ridiculous in this manner. I, too, have shared in this foolishness. We have said that, if you have followed us thus far, you are no longer the fool, and we mean it. You have found that compassion has led you to a willingness to heal, and in healing you have found yourself wanting a state of transcendence. This is the ultimate healing.

What is the real difference between your state and this state? This state is with you no matter who you are. In this state, the contemplation of oneness is possible, but it is not possible without the heart. Compassion must come first. If you see a beggar on the street, you go to him in compassion. You do not become frightened and turn away to seek enlightenment. It is by being drawn to compassion that you ultimately find transcendence.

So, where does compassion lead you? It leads you to undress before the mirror and laugh. It leads you to a place which you cannot imagine, and yet to which you cannot help but be drawn. It is not a place of forgetting what self is, or divesting yourself of the craving for meaning, or removing yourself from the world. It is a place in which you remember. It is a place in which you are one with your memory, and, therefore, one with everything. It is the memory in love of what is to come, what has been, and what is now.

If we cannot speak to you from on high, it is because neither of us is on high, but we can speak to you from transcendence, because you are in a state of transcendence but have forgotten this. If everything is devoid of meaning, so is transcendence, except that you have forgotten it is. You can remember that, if nothing has meaning, then the first nothing which has no meaning is transcendence. You have forgotten, in your acquisition of knowledge, that you come from transcendence. You have forgotten that the mind has always been in transcendence, or else contemplation could not take place. You have forgotten that no meaning is transcendence. In shucking meaning, as you have shucked self, you see yourself naked in front of the mirror. And when you begin to laugh, you are remembering transcendence. Who has gotten you here you no longer care. So, if you have cosmetically altered yourself, a naked you will appear even more foolish in this manner, perfumed, made up, but with every bruise and wart exposed.

You are what is before you. Your remembrance is your transcendence. Your transcendence gives enlightenment to no one. No self becomes enlightened. The master is not enlightened, because, although there is Light, there is no self to receive it. What has received Light all this time has been what is in front of the mirror. What has been in darkness all the time has been the search for meaning and self, that relentless search which would have taken you away from creation, compassion, and healing.

If Light does not shine on self, what does it shine on? I will answer, but you will stop grabbing onto my coat when you ask this question. It shines on that in which you have yet to believe, that which is most sacred, and that which is most embodied. When you debate who has soul and what has soul, or whether there is soul, you cause the Creator pain. Your eyes and mind are then turned away from what is the most sacred. If your mind was the most sacred, then it would have been the most pure. Errant thoughts would never have troubled you. If your heart was most sacred and pure, then unkindness would never have arisen in it. Hatred would have been crushed before it ever found expression in the world. If it were soul in need of being pure, you, being of soul, would not exist. The thing most sacred and pure, your highest expression, has been your body. What has been most sacred is that you are alive, that there is life. What is self? You may not know self. You may not know soul. You may not know essence. You may not find meaning. You may not know where love begins and where love ends, where it is in its center, or where it has lost its locus. But you know life. Whatever is happening, there is life. The mind wanders away, but life is still with you.

What little respect you have for the greatest transcendent thing! What little love you have for it. How you have tampered with it in an attempt to be pure. Would we say that the body of everyone in the world is pure because life is pure? Let me tell you, this cannot be so. Rather, we will say that the expression in body of the life force is most pure. The man whose legs dangle uselessly beneath him knows in transcendent thought better than you that life itself has found its purest expression in him. It can be no purer. If you see destruction and death, disease, deprivation, you are seeing purity, because there is life.

When you pass into judgment, what is the first thing which passes from you? It is life. What is the first thing that you judge? It is body. What is the last thing that you hold sacred? It is mind. If mind were purer, my friends, we would not need to speak to you. You would not put one thought in a more ascended position than another. You would not contemplate one speck of reality as greater than another. But you do. Can you reach inside your wallet with your eyes closed and find the ten dollar bill amongst all the one dollar bills that you have? Can you smell it? You cannot touch it. You cannot smell it. You cannot hear it. You cannot taste it. You can see it, because sight, being so close to mind, is what discriminates. And by discriminating, the potential for judgment, in a mind eternally toying with impurity, becomes enormous. This dalliance with thoughts of what is compassion, what is not compassion, what is self and what is not self, what is and what is not, is all of the mind. The mind seeks rest at some point in the living and flourishes best where life accompanies it. The mind detached from life finds no solace, and no nourishment. You cannot bring mind into being in formlessness. Without form, mind collapses in fear. The mind brings thought to being through form, but needs form itself to vitalize it. The form that you have so often thought to shed is the body which brings the greatest life to your mind. Your body is your form.

We see so many beings in this world whose contemplation of self- destruction is the most preeminent thought in their minds. So little is their love of the sacred that they seek to harm the body. You cannot have self, but you must always have form. And in seeking to harm form, you seek to cripple the Godhead. How do you know that you are alive—because you think that you are alive? You are a fool if you believe this. How do you know that you think? You think, only because you are alive. How do you know instead that you are alive? You know you are alive, because that energy coming up your spine, coming through your bowels, coming from your seat to the tip of your tongue, that energy like blood and like fire is irrefutable. And you know because, in asking the question, you have realized that the question is the answer. That which asks the question, "What is alive?" is life itself. That which has asked all the questions has not been the mind, has not been the soul, and has not been the heart. It has been the life energy which courses through you that questions. And in imposing the questions, it already knows the answers, but cannot say them and seeks to have them said by the mind, by the heart, or by the soul itself. But it must ask, and yet, while asking, it knows that it has transcended, for it knows that the question itself is the answer.

What is alive? You have known that this force coming through you is enlightenment, but you have forgotten. You have forgotten, my friends, that this force is one to which you have been most driven. You have thought that there was a transcendent thought, and there are no transcendent thoughts. Why would there be? All thought is wrought out of experience and cannot transcend its own origins. You have thought that transcendence was a transcendent heart. But heart and love do not transcend. In transcending they would turn away from healing, from loving activity. They would turn away from compassion and the Oneness of compassion. You have thought that transcendence was creation, but it cannot be, because creation, whatever it can transcend, cannot transcend itself. Transcendence is life. Transcendence is that which has no mind, no heart, no beginning and no end in creation. Transcendence is the sensation of life itself without qualification. Whatever you have thought life has sought out, it has sought out nothing and in that it becomes transcendent. It is content to be itself. Whatever being you have interpreted as being alive, you are alive first to interpret.

You can sit in denial of everything but the body which sits. You could sit under whatever tree you choose, but you must sit. If you know nothing else, you must know that something is sitting there, and that something is alive. If you leave with this knowledge and only this knowledge, what is to happen? What other knowledge would you need? Where has heart driven you, and to what has creation brought you? It has brought you to the realm in which all infinite things can take place. How do you transcend the ordinary? By this acknowledgment: all infinite living things will manifest themselves in creation.

Your feeling is that you must get up, but you must do this in recognition that your desire to live is transcendence. And in getting up, you must take your primordial step. It is a step without forethought and without afterthought. It is the first and highest step of transcendence. And in this step, you must know that, regardless of whatever you have judged as being true or untrue, what you have seen as full of meaning or devoid of meaning, what you have imagined self to be, all things become possible with transcendence. Every step you take is filled with the infinite possibility of all things. How can you exist in fear and self when you are infused with transcendence? What is there to fear? What is alive is alive. Can you fear death and the removal of what is alive? No, you cannot. Death is nothing to life. It is nothing to this force. If you feel life, you feel it forever, and you know that. Its form may be ephemeral, may dissolve and resolve itself into another, but you know, upon experiencing it, that it cannot cease. So, there cannot be any fear of death.

Do you own life? You are devoid of meaning, therefore you cannot own it. Who has given life to you? It has given of itself to you. Mind is thinking these things as you speak them. Mind need not know. You believed that mind would share knowledge when it transcended. Now you know that mind has nothing to transcend.

You will not sit forever. If you sat forever under the tree, you would not be enlightened. It is when you get up that you are enlightened. And it is because you find the expression of this energy in the infinite that you do rise. When all knowledge comes to you, you will have to sit under the weight of that knowledge. When you think how the sun rises and sinks, how leaves turn or fish spawn, how the human heart is born and dies, you have to sit. When mind ceases its chatter, when you know no one piece of the infinite realm of possibility, you must rise and move through creation. Whose creation it is now is not important. You will move through it. When you sit and contemplate your navel, you are full of it, you are full of knowledge. Your reluctance to move this vital energy, to feel alive and to enjoy life, is a sign that you have no transcendence within you.

It is time for me to depart. I share my love with you. Where do you wish to be now? Most likely someplace else. But that is your mind jabbering. Take a breath. Your breath is a better contemplative tool than your mind. Take your breath and know that you are sensing in your breath the energy within you. Whatever you have built for yourself, like sand castles, must be destroyed. Whatever you have used to adorn yourself, like the raiments of a prince or princess, you must remove. You must stand naked and laugh. Laughter is transcendence. And nakedness is always a cause for laughter. Where does the laughter go? It goes into the void. The void is a place where all things exist in their infinite potential, but which have no manifestation.

You have been laughing into the void; casting your self-doubt and your ridiculous searches into the void, shedding your selves, casting them into the void. Allow God to put this void to work like a sculptor.

In casting things out, you have moved toward transcendence. And, as you see yourself in the mirror and laugh, you know that your image is not the void, but the mirror is. And in seeing yourself, you see the mirror and thus the void. You see before you everything that exists in its infinite nature at once. As you see it, your laughter becomes transcendent.

We go from you now, but our deep heart is with you. Good-bye. God bless you.

PART FOUR

Passion

Preface

We bring you greetings again from the Source of all Light and Love. My name is Lenonda and here in these final two parts of the book, The Path of the Creator, we have much to do. In fact, these final parts are the most important. It is not because what has gone before has been of little significance—this is not true. We believe that everything expressed was done out of necessity and is derived from the Godhead without qualification. Yet, at this point, we must see that passion is the quality least understood and what most cries out to be heard in the human voice. It is what raises up the most human fears. It is why you look upon compassion as devoid of strength and the instinct for survival. It is why you entertain the idea that transcendence can be pushed aside, and it is why you see healing as something which is separate from the emotional realm, and why you quash emotions in order to heal. Unless passion underlies everything, the denial of your true motivations and the denial of the life force energy coursing through everyone will cause chaos in your world. We do not believe that the force of chaos is something people consciously choose in their desire to bring the world into peace. We do not feel that anarchy is a necessary step to the reestablishment of harmony upon the planet and to the destruction of imposed orders and rules. But, unless you embrace passion, you will find yourself in a state of anarchy. You will decide that all rules must be shot down and that a new order in harmony dictates this total rending of the established order.

Passion tells you that harmony demands a disintegration of imposed orders and rules foisted on humankind by the jealous gods. You do not understand this as yet. But, we will bring you to this point, for you have not been creating alone on this planet. We could rightly say that your fear of your own creative faculties has been cultivated by those who now create themselves. The only way for those of the Light to create is to embrace their own sexuality. When the sensual world slipped away from you in Book 1, Part 1, you found yourself in emptiness. You were devoid of true contact with God, true knowledge of who and what you are, painfully separated from purpose by the desire to search for and cling to meaning. You were separated from essence by the desire to instill essence inside yourself. Once again, we must embrace the world of the senses. If they are used, they can teach. If you shun them, you will not achieve transcendence. You will cause misery. They will come back to slap you in the face.

The desire to be sexual in this world is an inherent desire to create. Whether you see the act of making love as procreative or not, there is an inherent desire to create within it. We cannot and will not tell you that sexuality by itself will bring forth your creative power. You may be hiding your true potency in mere sexuality, and you may not want to see yourself in these terms. You may see sexuality as an addiction or, conversely, as something to be avoided. However, this cannot be the case once you step into compassion for self. Then, you must contend with sexuality in some way. And the only way to contend with it in love is to see it for the power that it is and to realize that this inherent power is God-sourced. In the process of moving into an enlightened sexuality, you also may discover through the body what it is most intrinsically capable of bringing forth: the manifestation of your own creativity. So, in this penultimate part, we return you to the world of the senses. You will soon see that, as in everything, transcendence compels you to acknowledge one more attribute.

We thank you. Now, center yourself in your most loving place, your deepest place, and as you read the book, we ask you to do it mindful of the God-Essence within you. Receive what is being said, and resolve to receive what is being written in love, for that is your only truth. Do not forget this. You cannot and you will not forget it anyway.

Lord Buddha has taken you, as best as can be described, to a place of enlightenment. Transcendence now, is yours. If you continue to read, you will have to ask yourself, what is the point of doing anything after transcendence? But, transcendence, if truly achieved, is nothing without the will to go forward with it, and nothing without being put to use. Transcendence apart from the world is no transcendence whatsoever.

And so it is incumbent upon you to proceed onward. How does one do this without slipping into the dull heaviness of the world you have so arduously worked to transcend? It is only possible to go forward in compassion and a willingness to heal everything around you, including the self which is as much around you as anything. In Part Four we will take you ultimately to your point of departure, to your view of the night sky by the campfire. But first, we must have you understand that your rooting to the Earth does not prohibit transcendence. In fact, your willingness to be part of the body of the Earth is enabling your transcendence. As we said, transcendence is not something done in a cave within some mountain. It is not done beyond human affairs or the natural world. True transcendence cannot see itself as separate and, therefore, must act in harmony, or it vanishes. As love can sometimes vanish, transcendence can also vanish. You may search for it like a man who has lost something in his pocket and cannot find it. One day this may happen, but we do not wish this to be. So, we ask you now to remember that you were once the fool and to read this with humility.

In Part 5, I alone will speak, because I, Lenonda, have been directing this book all along. It is not that I wish to hog the spotlight at the end. On the contrary, I wish to embrace you all as brothers and sisters and lead you to a point where you will derive the greatest benefit from the book.

So with God's grace and our best wishes, we will depart.

The Muskrat

☯ The First Gate

We welcome you to the First Gate. We are here not to mock you, but to teach you. We are not here because we feel a necessity to create allegory out of our lives, but we are here in order to share a story of our lives—a story also about everything you have learned so far. Seeing it as allegory is to diminish us in the animal kingdom. We disdain this type of story telling. We do not offer the drama of a life being cut, killed or starved, in order to explain to you what you need discover for yourself. But to share out of compassion, is a great thing.

All this time, we have not come to you to serve you. We of the animal kingdom come to you out of compassion. We care for you in ways that you do not know. No matter how many times you have hunted us down, tortured us, or deprived us of our food and our way of life, we are willing to come to you in peace and with offerings of friendship in compassion. If we snarl and bite you, it is because you are trying to impose order upon us which we cannot accept. If we hurry away from you, it is because we do not feel that our compassion has been received in kind. But we will continue to have compassion until you understand that we are here to share the world with you. We do not seek to dominate the world, and we ask you: is it compassionate to seek to dominate it yourself? This could not be, could it?

So often those who seek transcendence seek to distance themselves from us. We are so low to the ground that we easily display what you most want to hide. Sometimes, before you, we will perform our eating, our sleeping, our hunting, our foraging, our surrender and our death. And sometimes we will show you our sexuality.

You find these very disturbing. You have put yourself in a false place, but a place nonetheless, in which you believe that you must be superior in order to achieve some connection with your Creator. Transcendence, you think, tells you that you must escape your animal nature, or subdue it, even though you too are animals. So, the first thing you do is hide anything animal in you. You hide your defecation in pipes in small rooms. You hide your sexual acts in larger rooms. You bathe yourselves in quiet anonymity. You eat at proscribed times according to manners set out in detail.

Is denial of the animal energy in you transcendence? What has Lord Buddha said? He simply said that all you know is that life is going through you. Is it humbling? Are you lowly? Will you live in squalor? We do not live in squalor. Do you think that we have chosen small, mean, dirty little dens to live in? Who is making the rubbish? Who is polluting this Earth—the animals? Who is living in filth? Who creates the gray smoke and the stench of your industrial civilization? We do not. The plain red clay becomes our den. Who are you to say that we are living in filth? You would have to say the Earth herself is filthy.

But how you love to change the Earth, love to take her and twist her. And how you love to sit in this twisted Earth, to build your little towers, and then to look down upon her, believing that the filth of the Earth is beneath you. Bit by bit, you discover that those chemicals which you created, those substances in which you live, have brought you a polluted world, a world of filth, and minds of filth to which you are yet willing to cling.

Our refusal to join you in this world is not animal stupidity. It is animal wisdom. You have so distorted and corrupted the Earth's offerings to you that you have created a great distance between yourself and her. This is not transcendence. This is denial, avoidance and escapism. Perhaps someday, you will all flee on your little space ships. But, in truth, we would not wish this. We do have compassion for you, and so we speak to you as compassionate beings.

I am the muskrat. You wish to be closer to me so that you understand what we share. Well, I share a body with fur on it. I share that I suckle my young. I share that I eat all manner of food. I share a spine that is flexible. In all these things we can transcend. Could it be, at least in part, that what you have long sought in transcendence, those of the animal realm have found readily at hand? Perhaps, what you see from above as the limitations of our intellect has enabled us to achieve what is elusive to you, because the barriers of the intellect have not been present.

We go through life, perhaps, without the ability to separate ourselves from our root. We are close to the ground, are we not, scurrying about the Earth? And yet, in part, we have to say that this closeness has not inhibited our ability to transcend ourselves, because we can do this. We know that we are alive, but the ability to describe ourselves back to ourselves intellectually we do not see as a great necessity. Confess, that if you did not see this as a necessity, you would not have bothered to read the book so far. Do you not constantly want the intellect to describe self back to you? Intellect is rather like a perpetual motion machine. If our intellects are not that great, neither are they as hampered as yours. As we feel this energy coursing through us—the energy of life which we sense is beyond the single soul inhabiting the body—we respond in joy. Our joy is creativity. We respond in joy because life itself, this energy which works up the spine like a fire, rejuvenates us every time we breathe. It is the force that we know is ours, but does not come from us; the force that we know is at once tied to that Soul which is greater than our own, greater than what is in the body at any given time. We respond by creating. We respond in body to what is flowing through the body. This response is sexual. It is a response that brings us oneness with the force that energizes us. It is a response that is joyful and complete. In its own way, it is the response both loving and beautiful.

We respond. The sensuous world does not respond to the transcendent world. It is the living world, the world of body responding to itself in joy, because transcendence knows that its place is to join in love and not to seek separation. We respond by creating odor. For us this odor is beautiful, something to be smelled like a flower, but like a flower permeated with the love of life itself and with the willingness to continue to create in the world. It is a joyful response to loving life which is the energy of the flame. It is a response that communicates to the world and engenders other responses.

Well, we can mate this way, can we not? We can sense each other. We can savor each other's love of life. The beauty of the world is also the love of it. Because you have worked so hard, we can tell that love is with you in the body by that flame within you rising up the spine. We respond to it. We know its Source. The Creator has given us life. We respond in our manner by creating ourselves. Although God has given us this flame, it is we who create the musk. And in giving this back to our God, we are rejoicing in Her and She in us.

My time with you is finished, and I go. May you be prolific in this world. May you find the love of your children and your children's children, and may you understand that this is the love of God.

Good-bye.

The Dove

❂ The Second Gate

The Second Gate is one of heightened senses. It is one of beauty and joy; it brings you to a renewed sense of transcendence. The muskrat has spoken to you about the energy working up the spine. Low to the ground, beautiful and in harmony with Earth, the muskrat lives her life in joy and transcendence. The muskrat embodies the starting point of fire energy. This energy begins at the base of the spine. This creature's long tail is a wonderful instrument for receiving it. Dragging along the ground, it sometimes seems to be rooted to the Earth's fire. This force which comes from God must travel upward through the spine, as a vine shoots upward through a tree trunk, twisting around it and enveloping it. But, as the force comes, it lifts and drives itself upward so much that, if we were to follow its end, you would see us as flying high above.

We are a white dove. We are flying, indeed, above you at this time. The force which began at the base of the spine is now rising to the tip of the tongue. We bring you not only the taste of it, but also the sight of it. We birds manipulate food with our tongues. The nourishment that we take in feeds this fire at our base. Through our beaks, we take in the air which fans its flames. We soar high above your jealous heads in beauty. We are white. Are we all pristine and chaste? Oh, we would be the only dove left in the world if we were, and we are not. Our whiteness is not a sign of celibacy, and could never be. It is not chastity but a sign of our transcendence. It is a sign also of oneness with the life force.

When a dove speaks to you, it moves its tongue and tells you the flame is the acknowledgment that everything is moving in creation as a response to this magnificent blood-red flame. The path that this force takes must ultimately find expression through the tongue. This is why it is such a sensual organ. It enables speech to be sensual. It enables all the singing of the world, like the lovely sensual cooing of the dove.

We hover over you. We do not choose to say that we are elevated. So when we are at your feet, as we sometimes are, and seem to beg for food, we are not humbling ourselves before you, but sharing with you in the ways that we can. We bring to the world what it needs. Because we have flown above as a symbol for you, it is hard for us to stand beside you. We prefer to fly above you so that you know in your thoughts that this energy, coming from your root and expressing ultimately through your tongue, carries words on high, bears them aloft and out into the world.

You are commanded to speak of this force of love and life. You are commanded to share in the sensual world with others out of oneness with this force. To deny it will bring pain, because it is what brings all feeling to you. What is the feeling you have at every moment? It is always, at core, the feeling of being alive. It is the feeling which can enable you to make holy the spoken word, the cooing song of at least one being of the world who receives in joy that force from God.

We bring you Light and love, and we depart from you now.

The Archangel Uriel

☉ The Third Gate

We stand with you at the Third Gate. We are a being of the angelic realm. I am the Archangel Uriel. Do we feel this energy coursing through us? We most certainly do. For what you have thought of as exclusive to the body is not. This energy, which seems to give life to the body, gives life to all beings, and is not peculiar to the body. Does this not seem to be so?

This force is the initial breath of God. It is what was on the tip of God's tongue as the Word was spoken and you were created. Everything has been created, as well, from the spoken word, because it is from the tongue. Everything has been created from God's passionate fire center. So, as the Word was spoken, the universes were made manifest, and worlds were displayed in all their glory. The energy which you recognize as flowing through your body is the energy of body itself, the body of the universe, the body of all the realms, and is not confined to the mere physical body. Yet, you understand it in the physical body better than in any other form. And, as it rushes through you, you can respond to it with the physical body better than through anything else.

You need to conceive of your energy as that which is unbridled. When you start to hold it back, you create pain for yourself. When you do not try to limit it, and it finds expression, you will see it as emotion—emotion coming from the groin that wishes to make love, or emotion that wishes to speak love in passion, or emotion that wishes to envelope the world in love. This energy excites feelings of compassion, excites feelings of transcendence, and excites the desire to heal and to create, because that which is healed is simply renewed creation.

As you feel this force coming through you, you wonder what its expression should be. But first, you need to see how diverse expression is possible. The female muskrat, close to the Earth, and the male dove, high above it, wish to be in balance with each other. They wish to be aligned in joy with each other. They wish to have harmony with each other. Your expression, from the root and from the tongue, needs to have harmony and continuity, so that you can discern how best to use this force, since, as we say, without its expression you will become corrupt. At some time, we might be able to explain to you how to do this. But, for now, simply recognize that this force needs to be balanced within you. You need to have the wisdom of discernment.

How are you creating balance within you between these poles? Are you flying too high, and have you lost your grounding? Well then, the dove will come down to feed, if that is what is needed. Have you kept yourself in the dark too much, warm in the bowels of the Earth, but now need fresh air and sun? Well, come out of your burrow like the muskrat. Once again, she will find nourishing food only if she emerges.

So, at all times, it is necessary to feel balance. Which is more charged with fire, the masculine or the feminine? Neither is. Which is a more fitting response to God, that which is low or that which is high? Neither is. Which is the most beautiful expression of your fire energy, the expression from the groin or from the tip of the tongue? Neither is. Why would you seek to elevate one and to demean the other at any given moment? As you go through the world, you seek balance. Balance lies in the center beneath the heart. It gives you the power to create, the power to move transcendence through you, and the power to move this fantastic force through you. It is not the power of lowliness nor of the heights. However, neither is it the power of the middle ground. For there is no middle ground—there is only Earth herself. It is the power of that force in balance—a power which neither damps the flow nor is dominated by it. It is a power which allows fire to have its expression. It is the balance and the harmony between opposites. It is not what inhibits. There must always be the expression of its force in balance, or you will find yourself slipping into darkness and decay. There is beauty in being present with this fire, and finding its expression spontaneous and joyful.

You cannot stop the flow. You cannot live without a spontaneous feeling of passion. You cannot deny it, but neither can you coerce it.

We bring you greetings in love, and we depart in love with humility before our Creator.

✿ The Fourth Gate

H ave you noticed that, as you traveled in the first part of the book, whether in the exterior world or the interior world, you always thought of yourself as a traveler, until the point at which you knew that you are always creating, and then you no longer sought to wander? It can be said that at a certain time you reached a still point. And yet, what was this still point? Was it the want of trying? Was it the transcendent thought that you do not need to put forth effort? Was it a place where all things happen at once? Or, was it a place of not caring, of complete non-attachment?

Your still point, my friends, is Earth, and I am the Earth. It is not you who is traveling, it is I. I do not dream you, but neither do you dream me. And you are not dreaming when you speak and I respond to you. I hold on to you, or else you would fly away from me. I am your still point. This still point is my body. As much as the body moves, we are sorry to say, it is yet still. When it tries to escape Earth, it finds itself in trouble.

Do you not build ships to go into the blackness of space in hopes of making a better place for yourself, or to go on an adventure which you have never before experienced? When you do these things, you help to destroy me, since you are not doing them in love, but in the hope of escape. Then you imagine that you are beings of the galaxy or of the universe and are not fettered by the Earth whom you call your mother. And, like a mother onto whose apron strings you hold, you wish at some point to let go But, I cannot be your mother, and you cannot release yourself from me any more than I can release myself from you. You are not the beings from whom I seek salvation. Why do you seek release from Earth? Will it bring you transcendence? You will simply find that there other places in the universe that are just as tormented as the place which you have made for yourself on the surface of Earth. Do you think that you could, in your travels, seek out a place of holiness, of peace and of calm when you cannot create it where you live? Matter being drawn to like matter, you would simply seek out warfare, destruction and turmoil.

In the attempt to release yourself from body, you lose your still point, and you are moved off your center, which is also my center. You move away from it and into chaos. In your attempt to release yourself from the confines of earthly necessities and passions, you attempt to escape from yourselves. Your own bodies tell you that they need nourishment and yet you believe that when you arrive at a higher state you will not need to savor the food on your tongue, or to pass it through your bowels.

We are not here to torment your soul. We were not created to be your purgatory. We were created to bring love and to bring forth creation ourselves out of that love, but out of a passionate love, not a love which is harnessed. Yet you harness us and ask us to live with chains upon us. You try to pollute us—and you succeed. You wage your silly wars on us. You spit on us. We are not your mother, and you are not in your adolescence, attempting to break away. Who has told you that you need to transcend the gravitational pull of the planet in order to heal? We were brought forth from the Creator to manifest, in this part of the universe, a world of such love and passion that others would be in awe of it. Yet, here I am, spinning in the disease which has been brought forth from those in body who inhabit my self.

Why is body of such disdain to you? Why do you see the body in such ugliness? Why do you attempt to suppress it? Why do you mock it? Why do you scorn it? Why do you destroy it? Do you wish to show that you are better than the body, that you have transcended the body? Why do you want to violate God's wish that the body be something of glory and holiness? I wish to live in such a body. I know that through the body comes the fire, the passion. Without it I do not feel like creating; and without creation, what purpose would I have to live?

The Fourth Gate

Can you not see what I do? Can you not see my seas and mountains, the fiery volcanoes and the icy caps of my poles? Can you not feel me quake? Can you not witness me bringing forth flowers, birds, and trees? From where have you come that you do not understand me? Maybe you are travelers from a far-off place who have sought to escape themselves by escaping their homeland, and you have found me unconsciously. Now you see yourselves unconscious upon me and want to escape again. And, perhaps again you will depart and then, again, want to escape from wherever you are.

There is so much lack of love upon me that I cringe. We see and we feel, but also we hear your voices. These are not the voices of calm; they are the voices of disharmony and pain. You are unhappy with me. You will tear down what I build up. You will make little mockeries of my creation: plastic trees, buildings in cities which amass themselves into gray mountains, lakes formed by dams where there should be no lakes. You paint things in the sky. You send waves of violent forces through me while dismissing those waves that I send in love. You wish in your heart of hearts to do away with my gravity. Every technological effort is a prayer that you may all escape my pull, and go beyond the moon, and as you have not done this, it pains you.

Those who dance upon the Earth do so in concert with my gravity. Those who fly do so in the currents of wind that I have created. If you wish to transcend, you need not go anywhere. Your disdain for me is a disdain for your own bodies. You wish to see yourselves in forms repugnant to me. You wish to make yourselves into forms that are alike. But, where there is great sameness, there is great monotony. And, when you are unsatisfied by the persecution of the human races, you persecute the races of the animals. You drive them away from you, or you capture, manipulate and torture them.

You are discontent with the things that form, in body, has brought you. We know why that is. It is because you have not yet created, because you have stifled your urge to create. You have become jealous of my ability to make so many things and to have those things in turn make other things without redundancy. Yet, you may still see that I am not your mother, and that we are of the same family.

You may see that we are of God. You may see that God is one with us and that we are asked to make impassioned manifestation.

I have seen myself in a way which I have not before. For all that has held me down and crippled me has also made me see that inside I have my own flame. It has brought me to enlightenment. I am a being who knows transcendence. I see this flame and I will choose to use it, and bring it forth into the world in order to create. You also have been held down. You have not been held down by one individual, or by a coven of peoples—you have been held down by your own shame of the animal spirit in you which creates and procreates. You have been held down by the shame of the masculine fitting into the feminine. You have been held down by the shame of orgasm. You have been bullied and shamed into not bringing forth true creation.

I know that you will find the answer, but I will not wait. If I do not now create for myself, I will die. And I choose not to die now. At some point, you must understand that my first new creation will be healing, and I will not refrain from making that healing complete for myself.

I speak to you, and even if you do not listen, I will continue to speak. It is your hearing now that must become acute, since everything on this world is alive and speaks. I breathe life into everything which you see manifest on the planet. I am your world. I am your sister body. When you touch, you feel the vibration of the body. My vibration is not loud and not forceful, but, it is supple and strong. It is not weak; it is not still; it is ever changing. It is singing to you as if you are in an antiphonal choir. Why can you not hear? You will not be forced to respond in like manner, but you must sing a response.

I wish you only to create in truth. When you do so, bringing creation forth from passion, you sing with me and you do not bring destruction to me. But when you deny that love and passion work together to create in truth, when you create out of intellect, when you create out of greed, when you create out of dominion, when you create out of some false self, then you will destroy. When we work in concert, we create out of love and passion, we create in transcendence and through the body, and the body knows what it feels: it feels health and vitality drawn through it. When you share with me, we will show you how this is done.

If you deny your drive to create, you will be slaves, but you will be slaves somewhere else, for my body is weak and grows tired of you. As I have said, I wish only to live. And I have found my own creative source, a passion within me. Listen to what I am saying to you. If you wish to raise your own vibrations and to sense the fine vibrations of Earth in order to harmonize yourself with them, you must listen. They do not float through the ether. They come through the body. That is how transcendence manifests itself. Otherwise, how would you know transcendence? They are coming through the body and you must listen. Listen.

I am the source of all sound on the planet. All sound must resonate through me. You have not thought of this, have you? Carried by the air, all sound resonates through me. Carried by the earth and water, it resonates through me. Sound does not travel through space, but through my body, and so it will travel through your body. This sound will be the sound of your own awakening. When you hear it, you will find passion coming through you. You have not yet heard it. So focused has your mind been on transcendence, that you have forgotten the only vibration is the vibration through the body. This is what vibrates. The highest frequency is the frequency in my body.

If you wish to create, through sound, the Word, then you must allow the Word to pass through the air which is part of my body, in order to be carried out into body as manifestation. This you cannot do without. You play games with yourselves to think that your greatest creations are done in the next world. This cannot be the case. Your greatest creations are those which are done in this world, or left undone in this world. With sadness I feel that many of you have not been able to understand creation or your need for it. Instead, you seek transcendence without the body. You want to change your vibration, move to higher frequencies, and yet, how can you have frequencies and make vibrations without my body? How can you desecrate your body without understanding that it is my body, and still think you can pass vibration of a high order through me? All the incredible force of

Light coming through God comes through body, or it is unfelt. It comes not through the vacuum of space, but is borne by body.

When you see Light embodied, you rejoice. When you see life receiving Light, you must also rejoice. As Divine Light passes through body, it brings sanctity, beauty, love, and transcendence. But it brings those things only through the body. As it works its way up the spine, this primeval force from God enables all other forces to be. Nothing comes to you from the ether, my friends.

Do not be jealous of our great form. Do not feel inhibited by a great mother with huge arms to embrace you. We are not she. It is the Mother God who loves. She passes everything you feel through the body out of love for her children. There is no place where you can escape this. If you cannot reconcile yourself with the Mother God, then you cannot bring enlightenment into the world. And you will not, in enlightenment, be able to bring impassioned creation to life.

We thank you and leave. Know that we go with respect and love for you, which you have yet to feel. In the same way, as we know we have yet to feel yours. Good-bye.

☉ The Fifth Gate

We present to you the Fifth Gate. Deep within the Earth we dwell. As the Earth feels her own fire, we dwell in that fire in order to help it. We do not seek nourishment from it. We exist simply to guide it. We are few in number. We are fire beings. We exist inside the Earth, deep within her bowels. The Earth has a structure much like a spine—and through that spine courses the flow that you see as volcanic fire on the surface of the planet, a flow that lies molten within her shell.

Do you see what we are about to give you? It is frightening. You feel as if the fire will kill you. If you reach your hand into molten lava, you will know how fierce it is, and feel its destructive power. You are wondering if we are of God or not.

Remember your descriptions of hell, a place beneath the Earth of eternal fire? We come from that place, and yet, this is not hell. Who has proffered this vision of hell to you? Those who wish to rule you, and keep you away from the fire which can be yours have done so. Your vision of hell is a false one. Hell is a realm of darkness cast out in the universe where God is a far, faint speck of Light. Paradise is a place of beauty where a great ball of fire burns brightly, so brightly that there is unimaginable sunshine, radiance and joy. Hell is not a place of fire. Fire brings the Light. In recognizing transcendence, you recognize Light, the Light which fire has brought. This Light of essence, in turn, has brought enlightenment. Light, unable to illuminate one over another, and essence, unable to barter one aspect of itself for another, has brought you enlightenment. Fire has brought Light in the same way that Light accompanies fire.

We are in that furnace which powers your enlightenment. We stoke the coals. You have been afraid of the fire, because you have imagined that you will be burned by its heat. But you will not, because you are of that heat. The heat is the melting away of self. It is the melting away of the dross of the world. It is the melting in the fire of all the petrified grayness of the world. It will not burn you, because, as you burn away self, you see that you are God-Essence. There is nothing of you that will truly suffer in the fire. This is not your hell; this is your salvation. Why do you see the sun as blessing and see the fire as tormenting?

We will bring Light to you, but you cannot have this Light without feeling its fire. You have been told that this is hell, but this is the fire of loving passion. It is the fire of transcendence, the fire which will cause you to create. We have been holding it for you, because those who seek to enslave you seek to deprive you of it, and they are telling you to secure yourself from this passion, lest you get burned. But, what will be burned will not be you. What is you will be brought into Light. What will be burned are those old artifacts of self which you put into the fire. When you realize that in holding on to self, any self, you become insane, then you know that burning fire gives you over to great Light and love sourced through great passion.

We have called out again and again. We have asked that someone come and take the fire from us to give passion, love and creation to the outer world. This fire of Light and enlightenment, this fire which heals as it burns away is yours. You are, after all, of the body of the Earth. She did not come to tell you that she wishes to subjugate you. Rather, she wishes you to be empowered. She wishes you true freedom and the end to all slavery.

The next gate is the last gate through which you must cross. It is the most difficult gate. It is the gate in which you find your freedom, and you find the yokes of slavery gone. It is freedom at a price, but you will not pay this price. I am a being of God. I am a being of Light. I am a being of love. I go in Light and love.

☯ The Sixth Gate

I bring you greetings. You have arrived at the sixth and final gate of passion. We cannot endow you with the power of passion, but we can allow you to feel it and to have it unfold before you.

Throughout the book you have been concerned about what you have received from God and what you have not, what has been of your making or what has been another's, what has fed your creation and what has not. If you believe that all energy comes from God, you must agree that in receiving this energy you are cognizant of its Source, but you do not necessarily understand its nature. For, to truly receive the energy is to respond spontaneously to it and to bring forth creation from it. In the attempt to define God, you also define God's powers, and you tend to limit the energies coming from God. The force of God that created the universe is the same energy which now permeates the universe, and there is no true difference.

But God can reveal Herself to you. You can envision Her as bringing you infinite intensities and hues of Light. All that is not dark comes from God. And it can be said that even what is dark is the energy of God which has been corrupted. Those who stand in the Light, the least corrupt, least alter this energy, and become the purest vehicle for it. We can say at this point that you may perceive God's force as a brilliant, silvery white light or as a warm, gold light. In fact, all energies that emanate from the Godhead, from our One God, can be found to be in either of these rays.

What I speak about now, this fire of passion, is like the chemical reaction between the gold and the silver emanations of God. It is as if they were the chemical fuels which ignited all fire. When you see fire, the fire of passion, you know that all possible energies from God exist at the same time. Creation is not haphazard and it is not cavalier. God, likewise, does not create out of a single thought alone. God's entire being goes into creation. The fire of creation is the result of the volatile mixture of all those energies radiating from the Creator. This is why you see fire in the universe. It is the fire of heart and body, of silver and gold. It is the fire that can destroy, but also the fire that can heal.

If you are to be the Creator God yourself, you must possess this fire. If you receive it as a responsibility, you will be broken by the onus of it, because an infinite sum of energy cannot be controlled by you. You cannot dominate God. If you wish yourself to be a vessel for this force, you must realize that there can be no possible end to it. You must understand that whatever you choose to pull forth from this fire is as equally charged with creation as anything in the universes.

Why would you possess it? We have said that you are the Creator God, but did you notice that we leapt to this idea in the last node after burning the self in the fire? The fire which burns self away is the same fire which charges you with creative power. It is one and the same energy. The fire which burns all of your negativity away is the fire which charges you with creating in Light. The fire that burns brings creativity in love.

But, it was not such a leap after all. You were not then so fearful of the fire. Why? You are beings of fire yourselves. Although you do not sleep in the bowels of the Earth between the rock mantle and the crystal core of the planet, this does not mean that you are not beings of creative fire—you are. Somehow, in our retelling, you recognize this truth. But you have yet to own it, because you have been so burdened with negativity that you cannot.

You are born to this world to create. It is your legacy. You feel the rightness in our saying it, but you do not yet own the fire inside you. We come to you now so that you might claim your inheritance, an inheritance which has lain in the tomb of your parents. The seal on this tomb must be broken, so that you can recover this inheritance. If you do not act, we feel that you will be lost. In creating, you know that all things can be possible. But now, you must also know that in refusing to create, the weight of what is possible but unrealized will be overwhelming to you and will crush you. You must know that the oppression of living in poverty without claiming your inheritance of creativity will soon destroy you.

My name is and has been Prometheus. I am not the stuff of legends, but my name is. Forgive me for claiming this name. Perhaps in the future I will learn not to, but I cannot give you this message without attaching this name to it. And it has been mine.

Please understand me: the fire that brings destruction brings Light. The fire that brings heat can burn, but it can also warm your body. It is what is stopping you from freezing in the cold of space. You have been taught to welcome the fireball of the sun which keeps you alive. And yet, you have also been taught to fear it. Who has been giving you this message, and what shape does this message take?

We have spoken about the passion of creation. When you search your feelings, one by one, you find that passion has always been with you. We say to you that underlying all feelings or emotions is passion. Passion stands as the only emotion. It is the will to do something. It is fervor. It is the heat inside you wanting you to act or to think, wanting you to breathe. It is what closes the gap between what is created and what loves the creation. It asks you to love what you have created. It gets disturbed when you do not love what you see around you.

You can get angry. You can feel shame or guilt. You can be talkative. You can be mute. You can engage. You can withdraw. You can try to dominate. You can succumb. All this is passion wanting to seek resolution with creation, wanting to seek love. This is the fire that draws you to romance, that endows you with beauty, that searches the stars for God. It is what wishes to make peace between heart and body. It is what compels you to love. When it is disturbed, you behold wrath, hatred, and violence. When it is soothed, you witness efforts toward harmony, beauty, love, and peace. When you are charged with passion, you do not always see where you can go with it, yet you know you are charged. It seems a dangerous moment. Will you take passion into love? Will you take that person in your hand and bring them into your embrace and marry your body, mind, heart, and soul to each other? Or, will you strike out in hatred, not being able to see where love can be put in this world? Will you recoil from the world in hatred and anger and allow your passion to create violence?

Passion is volatile and does not give guarantees. The forces within you have caused friction, and this friction has created fire. Those energies which have come from God, no matter how pure they have seemed, now pass through you. Are you corrupting them? In mixing them together, will you create the passion that is a flame bursting out of corruption? Or will you create passion that is a flame bursting out of great love? We have no guarantees for passion. Yet, we have been charged with bringing it to you. We have given you back your inheritance. Who would stop you from receiving it? The answer, my friend, is simple, for you exist in a world where creation takes place in grayness. While you do not claim your inheritance, someone else may claim theirs. They are perched monitoring you, hoping that you will not claim it. They watch your passions, which are the sign that you are close to your inheritance.

How do you feel about this? Does it not spark a memory? Have you put aside this memory as being juvenile? We say to you, this is not the case. Pure passion arises out of this mixture in the Godhead, creating with wonder, beauty, excitement, and boundless energy. Yet, it is possible not only to corrupt this passion and direct it towards hatred, violence, thievery and destruction, but also to be passionless. It is possible to take the energy which comes from God, and without thought as to whether one is corrupting it or not, filter it, narrow it, take its infinite breath and squeeze it into a pin prick. Or it is possible to take its infinite strength and dilute it, to make its flow so shallow that there is no real passion, no creative fire, whatsoever. In this way you would not be able to create anything on the Earth. Instead you would be forced to impose order from the intellect, rearranging pieces of matter like chess men. But you would not have to face the fire of passion that will ultimately drive you to love.

Such beings are your masters. By not claiming your inheritance, you have betrayed yourself and have allowed others to dominate and control you. You can see your masters quite well—they are devoid of passion. If they do not erupt in anger, neither do they open their hearts in love. Instead, they know exactly how to fine tune a false fire to fit any situation. They seem to be reserved. They document what they do. They are good at rationalizing their deeds. They divide, they subdivide, they categorize, they limit, they restrict, they box in, they control. They invent rules of behavior. They expect adherence to these rules. How little instead, passion cares for rules. But, they are devoid of passion, since passion may drive them to loving creation.

You elect these people as your leaders. You have been taught that they are safe leaders because they will not passionately drive you to war. But have they passionately driven you to peace? They cannot do this either. This state of mind which allows those beings to be your masters has corrupted your own sense of self. Instead of seeking out those who know how to use their passion in love for good, you seek out those who cannot make a decision in passion, who cannot use passion at all.

These beings have been and are your masters. I have tried to liberate you from them by bringing up fire from the center of the Earth, the molten fire which was kept hidden from those who played on its surface. This fire does two things. It turns away all that is brittle, cold and dry, and it warms and illuminates all that is dark and cold. It brings to Light what has been in the dark, but it also may do this by burning it away. If you are in fear of the fire of creativity, you are afraid that it may burn something away, and this would mean your death. You have been taught that the fodder of passion is evil and you will lose the Father God if you accept it. Passion expresses the volatility of all God's energies in fusion. It is not the Mother God and it is not the Father God, but is fed by the Mother and the Father. It is not denial of our Creator; it is acceptance that we are likewise creators.

The denial of passion is the denial of God. How strange that those who seek to subdue passion so often turn to the Father God for acknowledgment. It seems that God shows favor to those who will not use this volatile mixture and bring forth creation, does it not? Some of those, who have been enslaved, have sought to emulate their masters and have corrupted all manner of God-given energy. If the light of the world is dim, it is dim for all the corruption of the Light around you. And you must realize that when you create in passion, in its purest state, it drives you inexorably to love, and that dimness will clear. You will be able to swim through it, to see through it, and to create.

It is our opinion that you have been slaves long enough, that you have been taught to fear yourselves long enough. "What if everyone decided to do whatever they wanted to do?" These are the words of your masters. "We must have rules or society will fall into anarchy." These are the words of your masters. "In order to be accepted into heaven, you must renounce all earthly things." These are the words of your masters. "There needs to be law and order." These are the words of your masters.

We have made a commitment. We may falter, but we will not fall. We will not fail. You, likewise, have made a commitment somewhere inside you. How can you be the Creator God, if you are afraid to go out into this world and manifest from your own loving center in joy?

Why do you accept the coldness of response from your leadership? You have been told that, if you do not create the truth which you know to be, that untruth will overwhelm you. This is the untruth of your masters. Because their names have been altered does not mean that their vibration has become music. The Earth, wanting to enhance her own vibration, must ask you to enhance yours, since you are singing with her. The Mother God is reclaiming her place next to the Father God on this Earth. When She does, passion will be brought forth, because those energies coming from God will be received in balance by the Earth herself and will create a volatile flow. Like the flow of lava, it will create fire and heat. It will burn away whatever it does not recognize as fire itself, but it will also give warmth and Light to the vessels which are willing to receive it. The Mother God, being mocked, scourged, and executed, is arising again. She feels unable to express in elegant words what She feels most in Her heart. Or, Her Heart is too profound, Her love of creation too deep for words to express Her passion. You see, everything you have learned is wrong. It is the Word of the Father which brings forth creation, and the Heart of the Mother which responds to it. If you use nonsense words to respond, you deny passion and love. Your words now must be directed toward creation. And your response needs to be heartfelt and silent.

You have been taught to fear the fire. You have been taught to fear your passion. How can you extend your heart and create in love unless you feel? From where is your motivation to come? Where does it lie? It lies in your passion, your will to create, the fire which knows all the forces of the universe come from God. Why do you think you would corrupt those energies and create out of evil and darkness, out of hatred, violence—because you see it before you? Are you frightened of a world in which there are no guarantees? This is the world of your will, so why are you afraid? Has your fear reduced the violence and the hatred? Has your chaining of passion been a success, or has your abuse of it caused passion to emerge in perversity, violence and hatred?

What if, in claiming your total freedom to create, you were to bring forth passion into the world anew? Now, you see that I only hold it for you. You must take it from me and look at the fire before you see that it is you. You must stare at it regardless of what is around. Find some time to be alone, take the torch from me, light the fire, and gaze into it. As the darkness is around you, you will not be disturbed by what is created or not created by you. You will see the fire, and you will know the you are that fire, or that fire is with you. You must go forth and create.

From where did the fire come? Did it come from Prometheus, from the Earth, from God? Do you care? You have got it now. Water turns murky whether it holds nectar or toxins. But fire is fire. It is a reaction. All fire is the same. It may burn away many, many things, but fire itself is always the same. It must come from some singular Source, or else it could not be.

Why do you doubt its heat? Why will you not take it? If you do not bear it with you, you will accept untruth in this world, which will destroy you, for all untruth is creation attempted without passion, and without passion, you will never be driven to love. So it is false creation, because it is without the potential for love. This is why you feed your machines, and they do not feed you. This is why you serve your institutions, and they do not serve you. This is why you are obedient to your laws and they will not bow to you. This is why you are humble before those in authority, and they do not honor you. This is why the Earth, a being who possesses great passion herself, is being hurt and subdued. When you hold passion yourself, you must honor it. You must bow to no one. To whom can the Creator-God bow? Only the false, mocking gods, who wish to drive you into subservience and ultimately into death, require obedience. Life, instead, means that you will not succumb and that you will take your passion and use it.

There is something you do not yet see. The willingness to act, to bring forth creation into this world out of passion, brings a gift. It is this, that, as passion comes and makes itself visible, it places itself in the Light. If the God-given energy which courses through you has been corrupted and has created a destructive fire, a fire charged with hatred or violence, the process becomes visible. It can no longer hide. The gift is that, as it manifests, denial can no longer take place. And, in acceptance of the passion which drives you to love, you may find a way out of corruption.

When passion is suppressed and the forces of God are not allowed their volatile mixture, they fester inside you, suppressed, unable to express, unable to ignite, until they finally explode. Your greatest wars have been the result of passion which has been repressed and has boiled over like a volcano. The gift of passion is that when you allow it to be freely expressed, it can find its way to love. This is the inheritance. In suppressing passion, the forces of God are dammed up within you, and inevitably lead to volatility, regardless of the corrupt will suppressing them. Then, passion erupts in a corrupt form, creating hatred, and violence, and strengthening the illusion of separateness through conflict between elements of God's creation.

With each breath that you take, allow the fire to rise through the voice and let passion seek its path to love. Like all the lovers of the world charged with passion, all the sensual joys of the world draw you ultimately to love. Passion is like a romance with what you have created and what you have brought into creation, and therefore is yours. The romance of passion will draw you to love. When you begin to break down your relationships into roles, you break down your love into roles, and when you recreate those roles, you are also denying passion, and you will fail in love. Accept that passion has no parameters. Does a fire burn according to a prescribed law? It just blazes until it is put out. When you accept passion, you find that you need no part to play. When you are told that you need to play this or that role in relationships, or that you need to change your role to another because you are hurting, you are hearing from your masters again.

What can you create out of passion? You can create sexual unity. You can create healing. You can create enlightenment. You can create out of the Earth herself, bringing forth from her, in partnership with her, great things. But you first must surrender to this fire and allow it to burn away every self that you put into it. To be driven to love by passion means that you must be divorced from all selves. You cannot contain selfish love in passion. Passion will ultimately drive you to infinite compassion, an embrace of the world, which is like the embrace of all lovers at the same time. But you must unfetter yourself. Let your masters play with shells of beings. Soon they will understand that they are not welcome and will depart. This is all you need to do.

My friends, I have finished. We are pleased to bring you to the end of this cycle, as we speak to you from our humble position. We do not pretend to have endowed you with your bequest. We are simply reading to you the text of the will. This will is the Will of God. And we are humble before this. Have acceptance for all that is to transpire in your lives and know that, if there is passion at all, it will ultimately lead to the infinite love that is the Creator.

I do not go, my friends. I will stay with you, but I will cease to speak. Let there be Light.

Part Five

The One Place

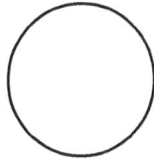

The One Place

W e bring you greetings, and as we do so, we say that this final
part of The Path of the Creator is also a place of departure.
Many times you have seen that, as we bring you each of the
beings of heart to be channeled to you, each in their turn must depart
to allow another to speak. In our final dialogue, I wish you to let me
be the being who introduces the one who, in reality, is the last being
of The Path of the Creator. This last being, whom I will introduce, is
you. For it is you who is to close this book, and we will tell you how.

Have you noticed that in the Path you have been led from
one episode to another through a series of gates? As one gate opens,
you find that you then need to open another. Onward you go until
you find that you end up before the fire, once again. Passion, in its
culmination, has swept you before the fire which Prometheus has
brought to you. This fire is the energy which surges up through your
spine, that sexual energy, the energy of being in the body. And it is
from this point at night when you sit by the fire alone and in contemplation, that you know creation must be yours, that everything you
see you must embrace in love before you can move on.

So it is that each and every gate is like a spoke in a wheel.
Does it matter where you start and where you end? No. We have simply picked the beginning and ending which is the most pertinent to
the greatest number of people. We have chosen to concentrate upon
your creative power fueled by passion because we found this to be the
most dreadfully lacking quality, the most imprisoned attribute, and
the most suppressed urge on the planet. The force of your will has
been what is most repressed, and it is one of your greatest gifts. Can
you not observe on your planet that, while you recognize you have
been endowed with free will, you create law upon law to harness it, as

if the potential of its activation is a threat? It is not a threat; in fact, it will be your salvation as a race if you are to be saved.

We have simply chosen passion because it is what is most needed. We could have just as easily begun with another gate. Consider the life of Lord Jesus. It was only after years of training that he took on his mission. The years of study brought him to a state of enlightenment. Through enlightenment, he found his passion. Through passion, he found the desire to create in compassion. Through compassion and love, great healing was manifested through him. And now consider Lord Buddha. He was born to great wealth. All the luxuries of the world and its sensual pleasures were given to him. He worked his way through passion to compassion and love, and from love, to healing, and from healing, to enlightenment. That was his path. Jesus, of humble means, needed to apply himself doggedly to his studies. But this was not Lord Buddha's journey.

Do you see that it is not important where you begin on this wheel, where you believe you have begun, or where you end, if you think of yourself as ending? We have given you the example of two different souls with two different lives, but they could have been the same being with two different lives. It is not important. Graceful movement itself through the gates is more significant. Beauty and gracefulness in the effort of moving through the gates is vastly more important than the beginning point or the end point.

Can you comprehend that everything is in cycles, and that nothing truly ends? The wheel tells you this. If you are always traveling on the wheel, just as you are always in one node or another, then it cannot be said that you are moving in succinct steps. The gates were never meant to illustrate firm, sequential steps to achieving some spiritual goal. They were to show you that everything needs to flow, dance-like. Where you choose to be is up to your soul and not formulated prior to your consent. How you choose to move, likewise, is not defined by the rigors of a measured spiritual routine. This movement, which you express in traveling on the wheel, only needs to be movement in grace. You only decide where you enter and where you exit and then where you enter again.

The One Place

This is what you desire, is it not? While seeing a beautiful dancer, you do not care as much about each succinct gesture as about the grace pervading the continuing movement of the body. This is the art of dance. Whenever you imagine that you must plod along, one ponderous step after another, you deny your own ability to move in grace. So, as you go, decide what is your beginning point, then stop and go back toward the center, then go out again into another sequence of movements and return to the center. This is you at your most beautiful. For, like a dancer, you will be coming out to dance, then going backstage, then coming out and dancing again, and so on. Otherwise, we in spirit will see you in pain, forcing yourself to plod through one gate after another.

Have you not read books in this life which tell you how many steps there are to heal, to be creative, to be spiritual beings, to make a model airplane, to be a great speaker, to find the right lover, to make a happy family? Whenever you go from one step to the other, you must remember that you are not living in the present time, that your mind, in seeking out the next step in your process, will forget where it is. You would have to go back endlessly to retrieve where you have been in order to understand where you are now. But you see this only when awareness comes to you. You do everything in imperfection, as much as you strive to be in perfection; you are loved by God, but nothing you do will be perfect. You seek to make pure and perfect what you have done, because your plodding pace makes you feel uncomfortable. Can you comprehend that? You find that when you gain one position, you remember not having done so well in another, and you want to go backwards and redo it. Or you find yourself painfully in a position where you have brought to yourself incompletion, and you try to go backwards and make your present position whole by making those prior steps more complete. And thus you are eternally going backwards and backwards, going over the steps until you get them straight. Your movement becomes regressive, which is the opposite of what you desire.

So, whenever you are learning about steps, we ask you please to unlearn them. Steps took you to the mountain and took you down from the mountain, equally futile tasks. Now we ask you to abandon all steps. Each gate opens up and reveals its beauty. Unlock each gate which opens into a new world and see that you can live in that world with those insights forever. You need not go forward or backward. At all times you are in the present. Wherever you are, you are somewhere, and you need not fear.

We have done a foolish thing, have we not? We have talked about dancing as if upon the rim of a wheel, going from place to place, and then retreating when we needed to backstage toward the hub. But we have not talked about what and where that hub is. Well, this is foolish but almost perfect.

What is at the hub of this wheel? Can you recall that in our introduction to the Path, we said you must be willing to read as the fool? Now, as we end our dialogue with you, we turn the last empty page over to you. Perhaps you can write down your thoughts on this empty page. Perhaps you can be the tenth part of The Path. But, we remind you that, if you do, you must be willing to be the fool. In this last part you may have some expectations that you are no longer the fool, because you read so far. You may expect that you can fulfill a role as a truly loving, enlightened being in the world because the fool is gone, because you have discarded the fool self on the mountain top. But our words now are this: you must be willing to finish this book thinking yourself a fool.

Do we frighten you? Are we frustrating you? Have you read in vain? No. Are you the same being you were before—the fool on the mountain top? No. You are another fool. Why do you imagine that any being of heart in this world, any enlightened being, any being who wants to heal, or any being who feels the force of their will rising up through their core, is looked upon as anything but a fool? You may have thought you left the fool standing on the mountainside in the cold, chilled by its own empty adventure. But now you find that the world sees you only as the fool. The world, whose attention was fixed on the noble adventures of the mountain climber turns to you with scorn and marks you as the true fool.

You must be willing to be the fool. Whoever you truly are, who is to know it? Can you share in enlightenment? Or, if you have reached levels in which you feel infinite compassion, can you in turn share that awakening with another? Who can know what spiritual achievement you have gained or what spiritual mess you have made of your life? Who is to know? When you walk the Earth as someone who has been ordained by the institutions of their society as an adult, as having arrived at a proper place among the peoples of this world, when you walk the Earth as a prince or a princess, you are a fool. The world and you, yourself, see you as empowered and in the right place, but, you are a fool.

For the world was looking at you, while you were looking at it from the pinnacle. When you are willing, despite all this attention given you, to renounce your achievements in this world and to go within the self, then to take what is left you and act in this world as a loving, enlightened and impassioned being, the world will turn and see you only as a fool. And between us, my friends, to do this is a most foolish thing.

You must be willing to play the fool. You must be willing to accept the judgment of the world. You must be willing to take a step forward, knowing that your feet will land without seeing anything of the world upon which to place your feet. As you go through each gate, each movement of the dance, you will see that every time your foot descends, it indeed touches the ground. Every time you leap up, you feel the tension of Earth's gravity. Your arms, spread outward in a gesture of grace, may seem to capture the air and yet yield to it. Your eyes may be turned upward and your vision may be upon heaven. This life, to any one else, will seem impossibly impractical, and you will be seen as the fool. And such a one truly is the fool.

Will you always be the fool? You most certainly will. It is simply that you will be the fool in a more substantial way than you ever have been before. You have only been pretending to be one and have now abandoned that mere pretense. You are now able to take on its mantle and its profundity. It is only after leaving the palace that the prince or the princess truly will inherit the throne. This is the lesson of Jesus, who abandoned his heritage of worldly power, who was willing to be born in the world a king never to claim the throne. It was this way with Lord Buddha, who held the reins of princely power and let them loose. And it should be your way now. The true monarch is the fool. You need not be content with being the prince or the princess anymore. Now you can be the king or the queen. These saints have shown you the way. Now that you can, take the mantle on your shoulders and put the crown upon your head.

Now you will be crowned the monarch of the fools. Well, it was a better position than the one from which you started. Where does the monarch sit? The royal throne is the hub of that wheel. The circle, being closed, closes upon the fool—for the fool defines the circle, being its center. As you go out to dance your dance, you will come back to it.

Who is the fool at the center? Do you wish to know anymore? Have you not been trying to find your true self and yet felt that you have failed? What true self does the monarch of the fools find? It finds no self. Where are the monarch's eyes? They are focused heavenward. What is the one self that you must in the end embrace? It is the same self as the no self. How can you reconcile that every self you seek is no self, but that no self, yet, is the self who sits in your center and defines your world, who sits in the hub and defines the spokes and the rim of the wheel?

The fool does not care to define self. For being a fool is not to care, but to trust. You will say, "What is the point of trusting? In whom am I trusting - in this no self or this some self who is only a fool?" But the fool is trusting in God. It is only the fool who can trust in God. Have you not seen that nothing which has gone before you tells you what is to transpire next? If you have not noticed that all your plans are laid waste, then you have been another fool.

We are sorry that the dance of the fool will seem to excite ridicule or laughter from all corners. The dance of the fool is joyful and bright, but does not seem peaceful and secure. At every turn, with every lifting of the heel and every sweep of the arm, the fool seems to be about to fall off a precipice.

You see, the false fool on the mountainside was afraid to fall. After all, it was a princess or a prince who was scaling the mountain. You would not have allowed yourself the indignity of a fall. What kind of fool were you then? You were a poor one. You were frightened at the prospect that perhaps if you fell, there was no God. So, you sought God out with great intensity, but you could not find God, because you were yet cleaving to the side of a mountain of nothingness.

The true fool, not the pretend fool, does not care to cling. The true fool has trust. The mountain is empty, but so is everything else. The summit is the same as the base. That liquid center of your soul has within it an iron taste like the water which has run over granite mountains. The true fool knows only that it is alive and that it owns a world, because it has created one.

Indeed, no longer desiring to be the prince or the princess, giving that up to the world, you must take on the fool's crown. Others' perception of you is not wrong. See that you truly are a fool, and must acquiesce to being called the fool, because what others teach you about yourself in this regard is always true. You have found your real self. And as you have, the world gives you a nod. You are happily enthroned there, in the center of your own circle. The beauty and the love you carry with you in your heart seems all the more obvious to those now who also see little bells jingle in the fool's cap with which you are crowned. You no longer scare the children, but delight them. You no longer bear great loads upon your back, but take simply what is needed. You no longer falter in your passage, because you believe you must accomplish everything step by step. If this were true, you would never take that one step off the precipice. If you had no faith in God, you would still cling to the vaporous mountain. And you are truly no fool in clinging to the mountain.

We are afraid that we have tricked you. We have left you in the place where we have started you out. The illusion was that you were not still the fool; the reality was that you no longer needed to be the prince or the princess. Now you are willing to be crowned in mockery as with thorns. The world sees the fool and sees the fool's love and cannot help but laugh. It is laughter that is yet love, for the fool has asked that it be accepted in love. It is the laughter of comfort and thanks. It is mockery, but relief that some fool is alive to save this precious world by being in it. For the world spins only around the fool; the fool is always at its center.

You must know that to be the fool again, no matter how far you believe you journey, you are always returned to the center. What happened to your princely lineage? Well, now you have a Divine lineage. You have shown yourself to be your Father's daughter and your Mother's son. You have shown yourself to be of the lineage of God. You have realized yourself as a being of Divine lineage by placing the fool in the center. You see in your own essence the nature of God. As the One has begot the many, you are begotten out of the First Fool. And to the One foolish enough to create all in love, we offer our humble thanks. God, as the First Fool, is the most loving and forgiving God. God, as the First Fool, is the most impassioned God and the most enlightened God. God, as the First Fool, is the most willing to heal. It is to this God that we offer worship.

In your humility and love for the Creator and acceptance of yourself as a fool, we ask you to take pen in hand and to write the final part of The Path of the Creator. Perhaps instead, your part is a foolish act. But we cannot close this book without you. It would lose its center. And so, please, consider whether you could not bless us with something to give the world.

Bless us with some fool's gesture. We must insist that, if you cannot write it, then you must act it. And perhaps that would be all the better.

As you bless us, we ask God to bless you.

About the Author

Theo was born on February 2, 1952, in Philadelphia, Pennsylvania, and grew up in its suburbs. He attended the Pennsylvania Academy of the Fine Arts, graduating in 1979.

In 1980, he married a pianist and soon had a son. While working at an art center in Wallingford, Pennsylvania, he was first exposed to channeling and the possibilities of direct contact with Spirit.

At the invitation of his companion guide, he began to channel in 1990. His initial experiences were overwhelmingly powerful and enlightening, in addition to being a great motivational force. His artwork attained new dimensions, and he found much healing in his personal life. His access to Spirit extended from the Creator, the Angelic realm, nature spirits, star beings, and animal spirits, to the souls of ordinary people living or dead. Theo has a special connection to the ancient ones who first populated the land of Pan.

In September 1990, Theo awoke to his higher self. The subsequent flood of memories, sensations, and heightened awareness which this brought put him in an altered state lasting three days. This experience provided him with the knowledge and impetus to move, with his wife and son, in 1991 to the small town of Black Mountain, North Carolina.

After three years of practice, during which he adjusted and honed his skills, Theo began channeling to the public in small groups and in private readings, and doing energetic healings that facilitate connection to Spirit.

As everything must change, Theo was divorced in 2000, and currently lives by himself. He continues to draw, paint, and write poetry. His interests include classical music and Jeet Kune Do.

Theo has given channeled workshops and lectures in colleges, bookstores, and private homes. His clients have included civic and professional organizations and prayer groups as well as individuals.

Theo's principle guide is Lenonda. She is the presence on this astral realm of one of the first created beings and may be referred to as a greater Archangel, an Elohim, or the orange ray. She has been incarnate in many places throughout the universe, but most recently in the Pleiadean system. She is looking forward to her first incarnation on Earth, which will occur in 1000 years.

Sometime in Theo's soul evolution, he gravitated towards the Archangel Raphael. He is sometimes asked to do service under Raphael's guidance. It is this Archangel who oversees Theo's group sessions and his channeled writings.

We are at a juncture in Earth's history when spiritual knowledge is growing exponentially. The old illusions are dissolving. It is natural in this context that established religions are being reexamined. Every religion has its truths, but each is also painfully flawed. It may be that people often lack discrimination when searching for the truth, since most are as yet unacquainted with their own true hearts and passions. And much channeled material is adulterated, corrupted, or has originated from the dark. The dust will settle, eventually. Meanwhile, some excellent material is also coming out, so that patience is called for. In this regard, Theo makes no apologies for the content of his channeling. Some of it may sound familiar, and some of it may be new. Much of it will contradict established religion and science. While no claim of infallibility is being made herein, and arguments and discussions are welcome, no reproach will be acknowledged or accepted. Theo, who is of the Christ Light, will maintain his honesty and integrity, but he has no obligation to persuade anyone else that he has done so.

May each of you discover your passion, and be led to your heart's desire.

Visit Theo online at: http://www.theosalvucci.com